Contents

Acknowledgments

This book has been compiled with the co-operation of several organisations, including other government departments and agencies. The Central Office of Information would like to thank all those who have contributed their comments, and in particular the Welsh Office, the Welsh Development Agency, the Wales Tourist Board and the Sports Council for Wales.

Photograph Credits

Numbers refer to the pages of the illustration section (1 to 8): Wales Tourist Board p. 1 (top), p. 6 (bottom); Garden Festival Wales p. 1 (bottom); Cardiff Bay Development Corporation p. 2 (top and bottom); COI Pictures p. 6 (top), p. 7 (bottom), p. 8 (bottom); Richard Leeney p. 7 (top); Welsh Office p. 8 (top).

942

Wales

London: H M S O

Withdrawn

T012279

20,081

942 Ref

©

Researched and written by Reference Services, Central Office of Information.

This publication is an expanded and updated version of a booklet with the same title previously published by the Foreign & Commonwealth Office.

© Crown copyright 1993
Applications for reproduction should be made to HMSO.
First published 1993

ISBN 0 11 701754 X

HMSO

HMSO publications are available from:

HMSO Publications Centre
(Mail, fax and telephone orders only)
PO Box 276, London SW8 5DT
Telephone orders 071-873 9090
General enquiries 071-873 0011
(queuing system in operation for both numbers)
Fax orders 071-873 8200

HMSO Bookshops
49 High Holborn, London WC1V 6HB   071-873 0011
Fax 071-873 8200 (counter service only)
258 Broad Street, Birmingham B1 2HE   021-643 3740   Fax 021-643 6510
Southey House, 33 Wine Street, Bristol BS1 2BQ
0272 264306   Fax 0272 294515
9-21 Princess Street, Manchester M60 8AS   061-834 7201   Fax 061-833 0634
16 Arthur Street, Belfast BT1 4GD   0232 238451   Fax 0232 235401
71 Lothian Road, Edinburgh EH3 9AZ   031-228 4181   Fax 031-229 2734

HMSO's Accredited Agents
(see Yellow Pages)

and through good booksellers

Introduction

Wales and England have been united politically for about 450 years, and the two countries share systems of law, land tenure and local government. However, the Principality of Wales (see below) has a history, language and culture of its own, as well as a distinctive physical, human and economic geography. Within the system of government in Britain[1] special arrangements exist for the administration of Welsh affairs, notably through the office of the Secretary of State for Wales. The Welsh language is used widely in everyday speech, and also in education, the media, administration, and literary and musical culture. In Welsh the name for Wales is Cymru. As people from other parts of Britain have increasingly moved to Wales there is continued debate about the best means of preserving the distinctive Welsh heritage and language. The Government has taken a number of measures to support the Welsh language.

In recent years Wales has been experiencing changes in its industrial base, with a continuing move towards high-technology and service industries; the country has been particularly successful in attracting inward investment from overseas. The modernisation of industry is being reflected in social and environmental improvements to areas left derelict by the demise of traditional heavy industries. The many areas of natural beauty in Wales, and its distinctive cultural heritage, have led to a development of leisure facilities and an increase in tourism.

---

[1]'Britain' is used informally in this book to mean the United Kingdom of Great Britain and Northern Ireland. 'Great Britain' comprises England, Wales and Scotland.

The Principality refers to the title of Prince of Wales, customarily bestowed on the sovereign's eldest son. Prince Charles, the heir to the throne, was invested by the Queen with the title of Prince of Wales at a special ceremony at Caernarfon Castle in 1969 when he was 20.

This book gives an outline of the political, economic and social structures in Wales including the Government's policies as they affect Wales. More detailed information on government policy on particular subjects is given in the relevant title in the *Aspects of Britain* series. [A list of titles in print is given on the inside back cover.] Further information is available in *Current Affairs—A Monthly Survey*, published by HMSO.

The Country and People

Geography

Wales is essentially an upland country, about a quarter being more than 300 m (984 ft) above sea-level. Extensive tracts of high plateau and shorter stretches of mountain ranges are deeply bisected by a series of river valleys which typically radiate from the centre of the upland area. The lower-lying ground is largely confined to the rel-atively narrow coastal belt and the floors or lower slopes of the river valleys. The longest rivers are the Dee, Severn and Wye, which fall to the lowlands of the English border.

Intrusive rocks of the lower Palaeozoic period are responsible for much of the spectacular scenery of Snowdonia (containing the peaks of Snowdon itself, which is 1,085 m—3,560 ft—high, Cader Idris, the Arans and the other mountain ranges of north-west Wales). Newer rocks adjoin the older rocks in both north and south Wales. These include the upper carboniferous beds which formed the south Wales coal basin and the smaller coalfields of north-east Wales. The largest natural lake is Llyn Tegid, otherwise known as Bala Lake (10.4 sq km—4 sq miles).

History

In prehistoric times Wales, like the rest of Britain, was populated by a succession of immigrants and invaders from mainland Europe. Celtic Iron Age immigrants established the first culture that is thought of as distinctively Welsh. By 500 BC the Celts dominated large areas of Europe, including Britain. Aspects of their heritage—

their language, legends, bardic poetry and ornamental metalware—have remained important in varying degrees in Wales, Ireland, Scotland, the Isle of Man, the English county of Cornwall, and Brittany in north-west France. For the Welsh, awareness of their history has been particularly strongly associated with their Celtic origins.

In the first to eleventh centuries AD, Romans, Saxons, Vikings and Normans successively invaded Britain, although most of the impact of ethnic and cultural changes was felt in England. Wales remained a Celtic stronghold—often, however, within the English sphere of influence. Conflict was frequent within Wales between the various princes, and unity was achieved only temporarily, either when a strong prince took control or when the princes united to defend themselves against attackers from England. With the death of Prince Llywelyn in 1282, Edward I of England launched a successful campaign to bring Wales under English rule. Wales was placed under the same laws as England, for the most part, and Edward's son, later Edward II, was born in north Wales and was created Prince of Wales at Caernarfon in 1301. This title has, with only a few exceptions, been accorded to the eldest son of the sovereign ever since.

Although Edward's measures meant that Wales ceased to have any separate political existence, they did not put an end to Welsh unrest. At the beginning of the fifteenth century a revolt headed by Owain Glyndŵr (Owen Glendower) became a national uprising, and Glyndŵr was virtually ruler of Wales between 1400 and 1410. In the event he was unable to inflict a conclusive defeat on the English, and his rule and power gradually declined. Towards the end of the century, when the English throne passed to the Tudors, who were descended from the seventh-century Welsh prince,

Cadwaladr, the way was paved for full union between the two countries.

The Acts of Union of 1536 and 1542 united England and Wales administratively, politically and legally. The feudal lordships of the Welsh borderland were abolished and Wales was fully integrated into the English county system; representation in Parliament was granted to the Welsh; and the English legal framework was fully adopted, English becoming the official language for use in court. As a result of these measures a process of anglicisation of the landed classes began; the landless labouring classes, however, retained their traditional way of life and remained largely Welsh-speaking.

Social and Economic Change

In the eighteenth century there were two developments that led to social change. The first was the spread of religious nonconformism[2] (see p. 8), especially Methodism, among the Welsh-speaking sections of the community, a development strongly associated with movements for popular education. The second was the industrial revolution, which gave Wales (until then a mainly pastoral economy) a new importance because of its mineral resources.

In the second half of the nineteenth century attempts were made to revive Welsh culture, which led to the strengthening of the stature and influence of the Eisteddfod, an annual competitive festival of music and poetry, and Wales acquired a large measure of autonomy in its educational system.

Meanwhile the Welsh coal, iron and steel industries had become important components of the British economy, drawing

[2]Nonconformity with beliefs and practices of the established Church of England.

much of the labour force and large numbers of immigrants from England and Ireland and so creating the urban centres of south Wales. In the economic depression which followed the first world war (1914–18), however, and with growing competition from other European countries, the major sources of employment—agriculture, coal, steel, tinplate and slate—all began to contract, and people began to migrate out of Wales, both to England and overseas. The population declined substantially in the 1920s and 1930s.

In order to revive the economy after the second world war (1939–45), the steel industry in Wales was modernised and a variety of light industries, including light engineering, chemicals, plastics and electronics plants, were attracted to the country. Despite a further reduction of jobs in the traditional industries, expansion has occurred in the high-technology industries, particularly electronics, with a high level of inward investment in recent years (see p. 18). The trend towards a decline in population has been reversed, with an increase of 19 per cent since 1945.

Population

The total population of Wales is estimated at 2.9 million (see Table 1), representing about 5 per cent of the total British population. The 1991 Census of Population recorded 2,835,073 people as resident in Wales.[3] The land area of 20,768 sq km (8,018 sq miles) represents 8.6 per cent of the area of Britain. The average density of population is 139 people per sq km, compared with an average for Britain as a whole of 237. The main areas of settlement are in the counties of Mid, South and West Glamorgan and Gwent, where

---

[3]Slight differences exist between figures recorded in the Census and those relating to mid-year estimates. Mid-year estimates are based on counts of residents but include adjustments to allow for a number of factors such as differences in timing and for people who did not return forms.

just over 60 per cent of the population live (see map, p. 4 of colour section). The chief urban centres are the capital, Cardiff (with a population of nearly 300,000), Swansea and Newport. There are about 35,000 members of ethnic minority groups in Wales, predominantly in Cardiff, Newport and Swansea.

Table 1: Population—Mid-year Estimates 1981 and 1991

| | Number (*thousands*) | | Per cent |
	1981	1991	change
Mid Glamorgan	541.1	541.6	0.1
Gwent	441.7	446.9	1.2
including Newport	*134.4*	*135.4*	*0.8*
Clwyd	393.6	413.8	5.1
South Glamorgan	389.9	405.9	4.1
including Cardiff	*280.7*	*290.0*	*3.3*
West Glamorgan	371.7	368.7	–0.8
including Swansea	*189.7*	*187.6*	*–1.1*
Dyfed	333.7	350.9	5.1
Gwynedd	231.3	240.1	3.8
Powys	110.5	118.7	7.4
Total	**2,813.5**	**2,886.4**	**2.6**

Source: Digest of Welsh Statistics.

Between 1981 and 1991 the population grew by 72,900 (2.6 per cent). The nature of the changes in population were similar to those in the rest of Britain, with a decline in the more urban, industrialised areas and an increase in population in the more rural, less densely populated counties. By county the changes ranged from an increase of 7.4 per cent in Powys to a fall of 0.8 per cent in West Glamorgan.

During the last few years there has been a small increase in the population as births have exceeded deaths. In 1991 live births totalled 38,079 and deaths were 34,136. The death rate, at 11.8 per 1,000 population in 1990 and 1991, is the lowest on record. Outward migration from the rural areas of Wales, common in the 1960s and early 1970s, has been reversed, with inward migration from other parts of Britain now occurring. In the period from 1986 to 1990 Wales experienced a net gain from migration of over 44,000 people.

The two new towns designated in Wales—Cwmbran in Gwent and Newtown in Powys—achieved considerable growth in population; the new town programme in Wales has now been wound up.

Religion

Christianity has been practised in Wales since the fifth and sixth centuries, when the Celtic Church was founded by native saints. The Church was later reorganised within the Western European Church, becoming part of the Anglican Church at the time of the reformation. The Bible was translated into Welsh by Bishop Morgan in 1588.

Social changes in the eighteenth and nineteenth centuries led to the development of a powerful nonconformist movement throughout Wales. Consisting of Protestant sects which dissented from the established Anglican Church, such as Methodists, Congregationalists and Baptists, the movement exercised a strong influence on Wales—a census of religion in 1851 found that over 80 per cent of those at worship attended a nonconformist chapel.

While it had puritan features, such as strict moral rectitude, Sunday observance and temperance, the movement nevertheless fostered a rich local community life, with its encouragement of choral festivals, eisteddfodau (see p. 71) and popular education. In the second half of the nineteenth century the nonconformist section of the community (which by that time included much of the business and commercial class) acquired increasing influence in Parliament and pressed for the disestablishment in Wales of the Anglican Church, which was finally achieved in 1920.

As elsewhere in Britain, there has been a decline in religious attendance during the twentieth century, and the influence of nonconformism on social values and behaviour is much weakened. During recent years all the churches have continued to take an active role in a number of issues of importance to Welsh life, such as the Welsh language and culture, and the significance of economic and industrial changes for communities in Wales; the churches are fully involved in community work such as housing projects, care schemes and youth work.

In 1990 there were some 220,300 members of nonconformist churches in Wales, including Methodists, Baptists, members of the Presbyterian Church of Wales, the United Reformed Church, the Salvation Army, and Quakers. The Roman Catholic Church, with some 60,600 members, has experienced development, and recently formed a third diocese. Although the Anglican Church in Wales was disestablished, it remains influential, having a following of about 108,400 members; it is responsible for the care of the country's medieval churches and cathedrals.

Administration

Wales returns 38 of the 651 members of the House of Commons to Parliament. In the April 1992 general election 27 Labour, 6 Conservative, 4 Plaid Cymru (Welsh Nationalist) and 1 Liberal Democrat members were elected. Special arrangements exist for the discussion of Welsh affairs in the Welsh Grand Committee, whose function is to consider matters relating exclusively to Wales and Bills referred to it at second reading stage. The committee consists of all 38 Members of Parliament sitting for Welsh constituencies, and up to five other nominated members.

Successive governments have responded to pressure for stronger representation of the Welsh point of view within the British system of government. A post of Minister for Welsh Affairs was created in 1954, and in 1965 the Welsh Office was established following the creation of the office of Secretary of State for Wales (with a seat in the Cabinet) in 1964. However, in 1979, after a prolonged period of public discussion about the delegation of further powers from central government to Wales, proposals for the establishment of a directly elected Welsh assembly in Cardiff were rejected in a referendum. Of the 59 per cent turnout, 20.3 per cent were in favour, with 79.7 per cent against.

Responsibilities of the Secretary of State

The Secretary of State for Wales, who is a member of the Cabinet, has substantial administrative autonomy, with full responsibility in Wales for ministerial functions relating to:

—health and personal social services;

—housing;

—local government;

—education (except universities);

—town and country planning;

—environmental protection;

—water and sewerage;

—roads;

—agriculture and fisheries;

—forestry;

—tourism;

—the countryside and nature conservation;

—ancient monuments and historic buildings (administered by Cadw: Welsh Historic Monuments—see p. 51);

—the careers service;

—training;

—non-departmental public bodies; and

—civil emergencies.

There are also certain responsibilities relating to the National Library of Wales, the National Museum of Wales, the Wales Tourist Board and the Sports Council for Wales, and shared responsibility for the administration of urban grants to areas of social and economic deprivation.

The Secretary of State for Wales has, in addition, direct ministerial responsibility for industrial policy and economic development in Wales and for the administration of selective financial assistance to Welsh industry. The Welsh Development Agency and the Development Board for Rural Wales, which are responsible to the Secretary of State, also have important industrial, environmental and (in the case of the Board) social functions.

The Secretary of State's department, the Welsh Office, is based in Cardiff, with branches throughout Wales and a small ministerial office in London.

Public Expenditure

In 1992–93 the total public expenditure to be undertaken by the Welsh Office is £5,809 million (see Table 2). In 1990–91, government expenditure in Wales was £2,964 per head of population, some 10 per cent above the national average. New levels of public expenditure for government programmes in Wales were announced in November 1992; provision has been made for expenditure of £6,300 million in 1993–94, with planned expenditure of £6,560 million in 1994–95 and £6,780 million in 1995–96.

Table 2: Planned Public Expenditure in Wales 1992–93

	£ million
Agriculture, fisheries and food	175
Industry and employment	166
Roads and transport	298
Housing	625
Environmental services	195
Education, arts and libraries	167
Health and personal social services	1,892
Administration	61
Support to local authorities	2,230
Total	5,809

Source: Welsh Office.

Citizen's Charter

Government proposals to raise standards in the public services were contained in a White Paper, *The Citizen's Charter*,[4] in 1991. This set out a range of measures to improve the quality of public services, to extend competition and choice, and to improve value for money for the taxpayer. Separate charters are being published for specific services in Wales. In September 1991 *Education: a Charter for Parents in Wales* was published (see p. 61) and in October 1991 *A Charter for Patients in Wales* was launched. *A Charter for Council Tenants in Wales* was published in September 1992 (see p. 59).

Charter Marks were awarded to three public sector organisations in Wales—Llandough Hospital (South Glamorgan), Companies House in Cardiff and Dyfed–Powys Police—when the first awards for excellence in delivering services to the public were made in September 1992.

Local Government

Local government is exercised through a basically two-tier system of elected authorities. Local government services are provided chiefly and sometimes entirely by eight county authorities (Clwyd; Dyfed; Mid, South and West Glamorgan; Gwent; Gwynedd; and Powys) and 37 district councils. The districts are divided into a number of smaller areas called 'communities' (about 1,000 in all). Around three-quarters of the communities have community councils serving as a focus for local opinion, but with limited powers in matters of local interest.

In March 1992 the Government announced proposals for fundamental changes to the structure of Welsh local government. The

[4]Cm 1599. HMSO, 1991. £8.50. ISBN 0 10 115992 7.

plans aim to improve administrative efficiency and cost-effectiveness, to ensure better co-ordination in the provision of public services, and to provide a system that is better understood by the public and therefore more accountable. The county authorities and district councils would be replaced by about 23 unitary authorities. Each would be responsible for providing nearly all local government services in its area. These unitary authorities could include:

—authorities in rural areas based on traditional counties such as Pembrokeshire and Montgomeryshire;

—single authorities for the major centres of population in Cardiff, Swansea, Newport and Wrexham; and

—in the south Wales valleys, authorities that reflect the form of local communities but are in some cases amalgamations of existing district councils.

The future role of community councils will be the subject of further consultation.

Discussions on the Government's proposals are in progress. A White Paper containing the Government's decisions is planned to be issued shortly, and a Bill to implement the reorganisation would be introduced as soon as possible thereafter.

Local authorities raise revenue through a community charge set by each charging local authority and payable by almost all resident adults. From April 1993 it is to be replaced by a council tax, payable by every household, and based on the capital value of each dwelling.

Economy

Recent decades have seen fundamental changes in the basis of the Welsh economy. The most notable features have been expansion in service industries and the development of a more diverse range of high-technology manufacturing industries. The traditional industries of coalmining and iron and steel production have been gradually contracting, while at the same time modernising and improving efficiency and productivity.

Government measures have helped to create or sustain employment, particularly in areas—both urban and rural—with high rates of unemployment. Special attention has been given to those areas affected by the substantial number of job losses in the coal and steel industries in recent years.

In order to establish and further sound economic foundations for the future of Wales, in October 1992 the Government issued a consultation document about the creation of a Welsh Economic Council. This will be chaired by the Secretary of State or his nominee. The Council will look at a number of economic issues including training, inward investment, support for small businesses, creation of an enterprise culture, exports, expansion of high technology, and diversification and expansion of the economy.

Outside the main industrial areas of the south and the northeast, agriculture, forestry and tourism are the main sectors of the local economy. Nevertheless, growing numbers of small businesses have been set up and light industry is being successfully introduced in many towns.

THE LIBRARY
BISHOP BURTON COLLEGE
BEVERLEY HU17 8QG
TEL: 0964 550481 Ex: 227

Some of the main indicators of the Welsh economy are given in Table 3.

Table 3: Main Economic Indicators

	1971	1981	1986	1989	1990	1991
Population (thousands)	2,740	2,814	2,821	2,873	2,881	2,886
Gross domestic product (GDP) at factor cost (£ million)	2,102	8,575	13,247	18,443	20,053	na
GDP (£ per head)	na	3,071	4,696	6,419	6,960	na
Personal disposable income (£ per head)	na	na	3,999	5,403	5,827	na
Index of industrial production (1985 = 100)	na	na	102.3	122.1	123.4	117.5
Unemployment rate (per cent)	na	10.4	13.5	7.3	6.6	8.7
Employment (thousands) of which,	962	939	887	982	998	985
Agriculture, forestry and fishing	28	23	21	19	20	20
Energy and water supply	74	61	40	29	26	24
Manufacturing	324	240	210	237	241	239
Construction	64	54	43	46	46	42
Services	472	562	573	651	665	661

Sources: Welsh Office and *Regional Trends.*

na = not available.

Note: Differences between totals and the sums of their component parts are due to rounding.

Employment

As elsewhere in Britain, the workforce increased during the 1980s, reaching 1.3 million in June 1991. The number of employees in employment was 985,000. Between June 1981 and June 1991 the number of self-employed rose by 51 per cent to 174,000. There has been a significant increase in the proportion of the workforce engaged in service industries, which now account for two-thirds of employment. One notable example is financial services where employment increased by 80 per cent between 1981 and 1991.

The unemployment rate has been rising in the last two years, as in the rest of Britain, although it remains well below the level of the mid-1980s. In December 1992 unemployment on a seasonally adjusted basis was provisionally estimated at 10.3 per cent. Unemployment in Wales has traditionally been above the average for Britain as a whole, but this difference has been reduced and in December 1992 the rate in Wales was around the national average.

Training

In April 1992 the Welsh Office took over responsibility for training in Wales from the Department of Employment. About £156 million has been allocated for training in 1992–93. Most of this expenditure is channelled through the seven employer-led Training and Enterprise Councils (TECs) covering Wales. Their role is to develop effective local training arrangements, and to increase the commitment of employers to training, as well as to stimulate enterprise in their areas. In November 1991 the Welsh Office published a document giving strategic guidance for TECs in Wales, which concentrated on the issues of education and training; support for expanding firms, including a Wales Management Campaign to improve managerial skills; support for inward investment; spreading prosperity; and serving local people.

A Youth Training (YT) place is guaranteed to all 16- and 17-year-olds who are not in employment or full-time education, to provide training leading to approved qualifications in skills which are in demand. In order to increase participation in training, two Welsh TECs operate pilot schemes offering training credits—vouchers with which young people can purchase further education or training.

Employment Training provides opportunities for unemployed adults to retrain or improve their skills, and is geared towards the longer-term unemployed. The Employment Action programme, introduced in 1991–92, enables unemployed people to practise their skills while making a contribution to the local community. Following a review of government employment and training measures for unemployed people, the Government announced in November 1992 that a new framework of measures would be introduced from April 1993. Under this, a new programme, Training for Work, will replace Employment Training and Employment Action. TECs are also involved in links between business and education (see p. 61) and in running activities designed to assist small businesses.

Inward Investment

Wales has been particularly successful in attracting investment by overseas companies, including electronics concerns from Japan, the United States, and elsewhere in Europe, and is regarded by internationally mobile industries as an attractive base in relation to the single European market.[5] In recent years Wales has regularly obtained about 20 per cent of overseas inward investment into Britain. In 1991–92 a record 71 new projects were secured from overseas, creating or safeguarding some 10,600 jobs, while 117

[5]For information on the single market see *Britain in the European Community* (Aspects of Britain series).

projects involving some 5,700 jobs were attracted from elsewhere in Britain. The estimated total capital investment promised by these projects amounts to about £1,100 million. There are over 350 overseas-owned or associated firms in Wales, an increase of more than 25 per cent on 1989–90. They employ more than 65,000 people and account for about 27 per cent of jobs in manufacturing industry.

Industrial Development Measures

The regional industrial development policies which successive governments have undertaken to overcome the problems of high rates of unemployment in certain areas of Britain have helped Wales make the transition from an economy based on the traditional industries of coal and steel to one centred on service industries and the manufacture of high-quality products. Regional industrial policy operates within a general economic framework designed to encourage enterprise and economic growth in all areas of Britain, and provides for economic help of various kinds to the 'assisted areas',[6] which in Wales cover some 90 per cent of the population. There are two types of assisted area: 'development areas' (where the need for assistance is considered to be greater) and 'intermediate areas'.

Regional selective assistance is available for investment projects undertaken by firms throughout the assisted areas and Regional Enterprise Grants have been on offer to firms with fewer than 25 employees in development areas to support investment and innovation. In May 1992 the Government announced that the grants for innovation would also be available to firms in the intermediate areas, while firms with up to 50 employees would be eligible.

[6]The Government is reviewing the assisted areas.

Grant support is also available to companies with fewer than 50 employees through the Small Firms Merit Award for Research and Technology (SMART) scheme. In the four years since the scheme started companies located in Wales have received 9 per cent of the awards, with a grant total of over £3.5 million. Help for innovation is also provided to companies under the Support for Products under Research (SPUR) scheme.

In addition, under the Enterprise Wales Initiative, grants and support schemes have been introduced for all small firms seeking consultancy advice, for example, in marketing, design, quality, manufacturing systems, business planning and financial and information systems; a higher level of assistance is available to firms in assisted areas and Urban Programme areas (see p. 55). Offers of Regional Selective Assistance accepted by industry in Wales in 1991–92 totalled £77.7 million. The Welsh Office is responsible for the administration of all these forms of assistance, and for the operation of the European Regional Development Fund in Wales.

Welsh Development Agency

The Welsh Development Agency (WDA) was set up by the Government in 1976 to regenerate the Welsh economy following the decline in heavy industries.

The WDA has helped to rebuild the Welsh economic base by attracting and supporting a wider range of modern industries. To do this it has concentrated on creating the right facilities for business; encouraging Welsh companies to grow and prosper; removing old environmental dereliction; and attracting investment from around the world.

Some 55 per cent of the WDA's £166 million budget in 1992–93 comes from its own resources. As the largest industrial landlord in Wales and with a property portfolio of 1.9 million sq m (20 million sq ft), much of its funding comes from rents and the sale of premises. Other funds are received from central government and the European Community.

Providing accommodation for business is one of the WDA's main areas of activity, increasingly in partnership with the private sector. In 1991–92 over 74,000 sq m (800,000 sq ft) of working space was started through joint ventures. The mechanism to achieve this, Welsh Property Venture, was set up in 1989. The initiative markets development opportunities across Wales and enables private developers to share the risks and the returns of a project with the WDA. There are over 30 such projects under way including the building of a major science park—Imperial Park—in Newport.

Some of these new developments, like many previous ones, are being built on derelict land reclaimed by the Agency. Some 120 sites now accommodate new industry and the WDA has undertaken Europe's largest land reclamation programme. By 1996 this will have removed all the significant remaining industrial dereliction of Wales' heavy industrial past. Under this programme, called 'Landscape Wales', some 760 hectares (1,880 acres) were reclaimed in 1991–92, bringing the total reclaimed in Wales since 1966 to 8,000 hectares (20,000 acres)

In urban areas the WDA has implemented a ten-year programme aimed at regenerating selected towns by combining public sector commitment with private sector enterprise. Over 30 towns have been identified as offering new opportunities for commerce and the retail, housing and leisure sectors.

Responsibility for the marketing of Wales as a business location rests with the WDA's marketing arm, Welsh Development

International (WDI). Since its creation in 1983 WDI has helped to attract some 1,000 projects involving capital investment of £4,700 million and creating or safeguarding some 100,000 jobs. Wales is now home to over 340 international companies including major multinationals such as Sony, Bosch, Ford, Panasonic, Toyota, Kimberly-Clark and Valeo. Japanese investors in particular have been attracted—Wales now has the highest concentration of Japanese manufacturing companies in Britain.

Firms from other parts of Britain have also relocated to Wales. In March 1992, for example, British Airways announced its decision to build a £7.5 million avionics facility at Llantrisant. This followed the company's decision in 1991 to locate its new aircraft maintenance base at Cardiff (Wales) Airport.

Many indigenous Welsh companies have benefited from the high levels of inward investment by becoming suppliers to the new companies. The WDA has developed a new range of services to advise companies on long-term development, meeting customer requirements, exploiting technology, improving skills, obtaining finance for growth and doing business in Europe.

In 1991–92 the Agency invested some £3.7 million in small- and medium-sized companies and assisted 180 in maximising the use of their technology. Many others participated in programmes to improve their managerial and commercial skills. The WDA's Eurolink scheme helped 36 Welsh companies to find partners in Europe for joint ventures, licensing agreements, product developments, agency agreements and research and development projects. A further 60 are in prospect.

Rural Areas
Businesses in rural areas are helped either by the WDA or, if in central Wales, by the Development Board for Rural Wales. The

WDA has invested £25 million in rural Wales through a variety of activities.

The main aim of the WDA's Rural Development Unit is to increase economic prosperity by the regeneration of towns and villages while retaining and encouraging the values and culture of rural Wales. Projects range from environmental improvements and agricultural diversification schemes to the development of new tourist attractions and advanced information technology uses suitable for rural areas.

Action Plans have been drawn up by 21 communities as part of the WDA's aim of encouraging self help. Some £7.3 million has been invested by the WDA in over 300 businesses in rural Wales and almost 2,000 jobs have been created as a result of this investment.

Enterprise Zones

Three of the enterprise zones which have been set up in Britain since 1981 are situated in Wales. The zones, which were originally planned to last for ten years, are intended to regenerate private sector industry in the designated areas by removing certain tax burdens and relaxing or speeding up the application of certain statutory and administrative controls. The three Welsh zones are in Delyn (Clwyd), the Lower Swansea Valley and in Milford Haven Waterway (Dyfed).

The Delyn zone, designated in 1983, comprises 118 hectares (293 acres) and is centred on three largely redundant textile mills. The Lower Swansea Valley zone was first designated in 1981 but was extended to a total of 314 hectares (775 acres) in 1984; much of the land has been reclaimed from past dereliction and neglect. Milford Haven Waterway Zone, designated in 1984, consists of 13 separate sites on both sides of the Waterway, a deep-water estuary; together, the sites total 146 hectares (362 acres). The enterprise zone at Swansea has over 200 firms, providing 2,500 jobs; and the Milford Haven zone has 125 firms, employing 2,000 people.

The Rural Economy

Economic development in Wales has also been helped by schemes of assistance to rural industries.

The Development Board for Rural Wales was created in 1976 to help stem the rural depopulation of mid-Wales. It operates in Powys and in the districts of Ceredigion in Dyfed and Meirionnydd in Gwynedd. It aims to create a thriving and self-sustaining economy through providing factories, advisory services, enterprise training, financial incentives to industry and a social development programme.

The Rural Initiative was launched in 1991 to assist in the aim of creating a self-supporting market economy in rural Wales, and includes support for agriculture and farm diversification, financial assistance for those industries which are broadening the employment base, training programmes, the provision of affordable housing, and the conservation and enhancement of the natural heritage of rural Wales. Under the Initiative, additional measures of support for rural areas have included an extra £12 million for rural housing in 1992–93, which along with existing programmes will lead to over 1,200 new homes being built. In addition to a £2.2 million increase in the Development Board's funding, the Welsh Development Agency will increase its expenditure in rural Wales by £7.5 million to £32.5 million. The Initiative also includes an increase of £3 million in funding for the Countryside Council for Wales (see p. 49), and spending of £430,000 by the Wales Tourist Board on rural projects and marketing. An important element of the Rural Initiative is the establishment of a competitive programme of local authority capital projects designed for the benefit of rural communities. Social as well as economic and environmental schemes are considered, and for 1991–92 the Secretary of State allocated £5 million.

Manufacturing, Construction and Service Industries

In recent years the output of the production and construction industries has grown, and the increase has been above the level for Britain as a whole. Between 1985 and 1990 output in Wales rose by 23 per cent, although in 1991 it fell by 4.8 per cent, reflecting the effects of the recession. Table 4 gives statistics for 1988–91 for a number of the main sectors. They indicate that above-average growth in output has occurred in several sectors including electrical and instrument engineering; food, drink and tobacco; and paper, printing and publishing.

The chief industrial areas are in south Wales, in the counties of Mid, South and West Glamorgan, and Gwent, where most of the steel industry and numerous newer industries are located. However, north Wales is attracting a considerable amount of new industry, particularly in the north-east around Wrexham and Deeside, and increasingly in the north-west, with the improved communications afforded by the upgrading of the coastal road, the A55 (see p. 44). Light industry has also been attracted to the towns in the rural areas in mid- and north Wales.

Manufacturing

Electronics has been one of the main growth manufacturing sectors in Wales, with many new high-technology businesses being established. Over 23,000 people are employed in electronics. The consumer electronics industry has developed particularly strongly in

Table 4: Index of Industrial Production
1985 = 100.

	1988	1989	1990	1991
Energy and water supply	96.1	92.4	87.3	87.4
of which:				
Coal and coke	93	80	70	56
Mineral oil and natural gas	99	97	89	104
Gas, electricity, other energy and water supply	96	100	102	102
Manufacturing	127.8	131.1	134.1	126.7
of which:				
Metal manufacture	130	131	117	111
Chemicals and man-made fibres	117	114	114	100
Mechanical engineering	106	108	97	88
Electrical and instrument engineering	143	146	153	152
Transport (including motor vehicles)	122	122	139	126
Food, drink and tobacco	119	135	155	151
Textiles, leather, footwear and clothing	102	111	126	118
Paper, printing and publishing	140	152	171	168
Construction	120.5	135.0	139.5	129.8

Source: Welsh Office.

Wales, which accounts for over 20 per cent of employment in this sector in Britain. Several major factories produce colour television sets, video recorders, microwave ovens and other products. Manufacture of components for these products is a rapidly developing activity.

There have been a number of developments in other areas of manufacturing as investors from overseas have been attracted by several factors, such as a skilled labour force, modern infrastructure, government incentives (see p. 19), and the spacious environment which Wales offers. Major projects include the expansion by Ford Motors of its engine plant, at a cost of over £600 million, creating or safeguarding 2,500 jobs in Bridgend and Swansea. In 1989 Robert Bosch of Germany announced investment of £100 million in a car-component production plant at Miskin, north-west of Cardiff, which will employ over 1,200 people. In Deeside, Toyota is investing £140 million in building a plant which will produce 200,000 engines a year, creating 300 jobs. The automotive industry is increasingly important in Wales, and now employs 16,000 people in 150 companies.

Wales has also become a centre for concentrations of more specialised industry. The cosmetics industry, built around investment by companies such as Wella and L'Oreal, now employs 15,000 people, with a further 15,000 employed in associated industries. This sector continues to expand, with the construction of a new factory for Alberto Culver in Swansea and the establishment of Crabtree and Evelyn's European manufacturing base in Llantrisant.

Over 40 Japanese companies have operations in Wales—one of the biggest regional concentrations in Europe—employing some 12,000 people; among the companies are Sony, Panasonic,

Matsushita, Hitachi, Brother and Aiwa. Companies from other parts of the world making inward investments include Euro DPC and Mitel from North America, and Valeo and Staedtler from elsewhere in Europe. The job opportunities arising from these new projects and expansions have substantially offset the losses in iron, steel and coalmining.

Wales continues to account for about a third of steel production in Britain. The plants are located mostly in industrial south Wales; the main products are steel sheet and strip tinplate. In recent years the industry has undergone extensive restructuring and modernisation aimed at improving productivity and reducing costs. There has been large-scale investment; for example, in 1986 a hot strip mill was refurbished at Port Talbot at a cost of £171 million, and £50 million has been invested in the Trostre tinplate works at Llanelli. British Steel plc's steelworks at Llanwern (Gwent) and Port Talbot are among the most modern and efficient in Europe, and both have received substantial investment in continuous casting facilities.

Aluminium manufacture increased in importance in Wales following the construction of a major smelter in Anglesey between 1968 and 1970. A rolling mill, the biggest of its kind in Europe, was inaugurated in Swansea in 1978.

Construction

The construction industry employed some 42,000 people in 1991. An extensive factory building programme is in progress (see p. 21) and the industry has also benefited from urban regeneration programmes, such as the development of Cardiff Bay (see p. 57) and the construction of the site for the garden festival at Ebbw Vale (see

p. 33). A new International Arena and World Trade centre is being built in Cardiff (see p. 33).

Service Industries

The service industries experienced an overall rise in employment of 99,000 (18 per cent) in the period 1981–91. Some 660,000 people were employed in service industries in Wales in 1991, accounting for 67 per cent of employees in employment, compared with 60 per cent in 1981 and 49 per cent in 1971. The most marked growth has been in financial and business services, and leisure services.

In June 1991 the major service sectors in Wales had the following numbers of people in employment (excluding the self-employed):

—banking, insurance, finance and business services, 90,000;

—wholesaling, retail distribution, hotels and catering, and repairs, 189,000;

—transport and communications, 53,000;

—public administration, defence, education, health, and other services, 328,000.

Financial Services

Wales is developing strongly as a financial services centre. In addition to the local companies in this sector, and the large offices of the major accountancy firms, a number of companies have made significant inward investments. Chemical Bank was one of the first to locate its operations in Wales, and in recent years it has been followed by the Trustee Savings Bank, National Provident (which has a 500-job project in Cardiff), and the merchant bank Rothschilds. Most recently the Prudential chose Cardiff as the location for the regional service centre for its general insurance business, involving 200 jobs. As well as generating many jobs in its own right, the financial sector is providing considerable support for the industrial developments in Wales.

Tourism

The tourism industry in Wales has expanded substantially in recent years, and is estimated to employ some 95,000 people, with annual earnings of over £1,250 million. The culture, language and heritage of Wales, combined with its fine countryside (including three National Parks) and coastal resorts, make it particularly attractive to many tourists, especially those who enjoy outdoor holidays.

Castles and historic places are among the main attractions for tourists in Wales. Many monuments are in the care of Cadw: Welsh Historic Monuments, which is responsible for their conservation and promotion (see p. 51). Increasingly there are tourist attractions based on exploration of the country's heritage. Many take a special interest in narrow-gauge steam railways. Wildlife parks and leisure centres have been established recently, and the many cultural events include traditional folk and music festivals such as the eisteddfodau (see p. 71).

The Wales Tourist Board seeks to develop and market tourism in ways which will yield the optimum economic and social benefit to the people of Wales. Implicit within this objective is the need:

—to sustain and promote the culture of Wales and the Welsh language; and

—to safeguard the natural environment and the built environment.

In order to achieve its aims, the Board works in partnership with statutory agencies, local authorities, the private sector and other bodies.

In 1991–92 the Board approved 258 projects, assisting them with £4.2 million, and generating a total capital investment of £23.8 million. An estimated 850 full-time-equivalent jobs were created as a result. The Board has a five-year Tourism Development Strategy, launched in 1988, centred in resorts, historic towns and tourism action programme areas and communities. By March 1992, under this strategy, it had allocated £14.8 million of financial assistance on capital investment of £120 million on 778 tourism-related projects, with an associated 2,650 full-time equivalent jobs. While Wales has a large share of domestic tourism, it has only 4 per cent of the overseas visitor market in Britain. During 1992 the Board was granted overseas marketing powers similar to those that apply in Scotland. Working with the British Tourist Authority, it will now focus more of its marketing activity on key overseas markets. Some 8.7 million domestic tourist trips (holidays, business trips and visits to friends and relatives) were made to Wales in 1991. Expenditure by domestic visitors in 1991 was £900 million; overseas visitors spent an estimated £120 million, while it is estimated that a further £270 million was generated by day visitors.

To improve facilities for tourism, the Board is tackling the shortage of good quality large hotels, helping to upgrade traditional resorts, and marketing the south Wales valleys as a tourist region. In 1992 the Board launched a £7.5 million three-year major domestic marketing initiative to enhance the image of Wales as a tourist destination including using, for the first time, television advertising.

There have been considerable improvements over recent years in standards of holiday accommodation. The Board operates an annual programme of inspection for all sectors of accommodation. Hotels, guest houses and farmhouses are classified and graded according to the British Tourist Authority's Crown Classification and grading scheme. Inspection and grading are voluntary. Over 5,000 establishments are inspected annually in Wales on behalf of the Board.

Business Facilities

With the completion of the St David's Hall conference centre, Cardiff has joined the group of major British cities providing modern and extensive facilities for conferences (both domestic and international). The Cardiff International Arena and World Trade Centre, being built in the city, is supported by £3 million of urban development grant.

Rhondda Heritage Park

The first stage of the planned heritage park in the Rhondda valley in Mid Glamorgan, a visitors' centre, was opened in 1989. The park, on the site of a former colliery, is scheduled for completion in 1993, and will include a re-created mining village. Over £2 million of Urban Programme funding has been spent to develop it over the first three years, and grants of £200,000 have been paid by the Wales Tourist Board.

Garden Festival

The National Garden Festival Wales, which was held in spring and summer 1992 at Ebbw Vale, was a major national tourism and leisure event and attracted two million visitors. It formed an important part of the Programme for the Valleys, which aims to improve the economic, social and environmental conditions of the south Wales valleys (see p. 56). The Government provided over £20 million of derelict land grant to reclaim the site with an additional £19 million from the Urban Programme towards the cost of the festival.

In the longer term, the site will serve as a focus for economic growth in the area. Some 32 hectares (79 acres) will be developed to include new housing, a technology park, a business park, a village centre and retail developments.

Power of Wales
A major new attraction has been developed by the National Museum of Wales and the electricity generating authorities in Snowdonia. With assistance from the Wales Tourist Board, an exhibition and associated underground tour, Power of Wales, has been established at the National Museum of Wales' centre in Llanberis, to link up with the Dinorwig pumped-storage power scheme (see p. 36).

Energy and Water Supplies

Coal

Output of coal and coke in Wales has fallen substantially in recent years, reflecting the closure of many collieries. In 1992 British Coal employed some 1,300 workers in its deep-mine operations. Small private mines in south Wales employ around 800 people, with a further 500 being employed in associated washing/blending operations. In addition, 1,300 more are employed in Wales in opencast operations.

As part of the rationalisation of the coal industry announced in October 1992, two of the four remaining British Coal mines in Wales are expected to be closed early in 1993 and the Point of Ayr mine in north Wales is to be examined as part of a wide-ranging review of the coal industry in Great Britain. The remaining mine, Tower, near Aberdare, will remain open.

Coal Mine Closures

The Government has announced a number of measures for areas affected by the proposals for the rationalisation of the coal industry announced in October 1992. Up to £4.8 million is being provided for employment and training measures. To encourage regeneration of the areas affected, a special allocation of £2.5 million is being made available in 1992–93 under the Urban Programme. In addition, grants from the European Regional Development Fund are expected to be available for a substantial number of new projects in these areas.

Restoration of Mining Sites

The cost of opencast operations has been reduced by the increased size of earth-moving machinery. This helps to meet expenditure on land restoration. Safeguards protect the public interest and the environment during opencast mining. After the completion of coaling operations, the Welsh Office Agriculture Department manages the land on behalf of British Coal Opencast for five years during rehabilitation. Since 1942 over 10,000 hectares (25,000 acres) of land in south Wales have been restored.

Oil

Wales has three oil refineries, representing about one-fifth of Britain's oil refining capacity: Pembroke (Texaco), with an annual distillation capacity of 9.1 million tonnes; Milford Haven (Gulf Oil), 5.6 million tonnes; and Milford Haven (Elf), 5.1 million tonnes. A 423-km (263-mile) pipeline runs from Milford Haven to the Midlands and Manchester.

Electricity

Power stations in Wales include two nuclear power stations, at Trawsfynydd and Wylfa (both in Gwynedd), coal-fired plants at Aberthaw (South Glamorgan) and Uskmouth (Gwent), a number of small hydro-electric plants and a pumped-storage station at Ffestiniog (Gwynedd). The pumped-storage station at Dinorwig (Gwynedd), which is the largest of its type in Europe, began operating in 1983 and has an average generated output of 1,728 megawatts (MW). When Dinorwig is required to generate electricity (at periods of peak demand), up to 6.6 million cubic metres (1,450 million gallons) of water flow from a mountain reservoir,

passing down within the mountain, to drive the power station turbines. Its quickest response rate (1,320 MW in 10 seconds) is faster
than any other pumped-storage station in the world.

The electricity supply industry in Wales consists of the three
main generating companies (the non-nuclear National Power and
PowerGen and the publicly owned Nuclear Electric plc—all three
covering England and Wales), the National Grid Company (which
also covers England and Wales), and two regional electricity companies (RECs). Distribution and supply in Wales are the business
of the RECs—South Wales Electricity and the North Wales
Electricity Board.

Renewable Sources of Energy

Among the projects at National Wind Power's wind energy
demonstration centre at Carmarthen Bay (Dyfed) are two horizon-
tal axis 300 kilowatt (kW) turbines and two vertical axis machines,
inaugurated in 1986 and 1990, with rated powers of 130 kW and
500 kW respectively. The Government, National Power and the
Wind Energy Group aim to collaborate on an experimental windfarm at Llangwyryfon (Dyfed). A commercial windfarm is being
built at Llandinam in Powys. With a total power capacity of 31
MW, it will be one of the largest in Europe.

The Severn estuary is one of the best potential sites for tidal
power in the world as a result of its exceptionally high tidal range.
The former Department of Energy (now the Department of Trade
and Industry) has funded, with the Severn Tidal Power Group
(STPG—a private sector consortium) and the electricity supply
industry, a study costing £4.2 million into the viability of a Severn
tidal barrage which would be 16 km (10 miles) in length. Further
regional studies into the impact of a barrage are to be part-funded

by the Government. An STPG report on public response to the barrage proposal has been published. The STPG recommends further ecological and regional studies. It also recommends early organisational studies, including local planning and overall estuary management. However, much additional work is necessary, particularly on the environmental aspects, before an overall view on the project's future is taken.

At Rhayader (Powys) a village of passive solar designed houses has been built. The dwellings are lightweight, durable and with low maintenance costs. Their large south-facing windows collect solar heat.

The Centre for Alternative Technology, a voluntary body, has a permanent working demonstration of various applications of renewable energy sources at its site at Machynlleth (Powys), including a water-powered cliff railway.

Water

The Water Act 1989 privatised the utility functions of the ten former water authorities in England and Wales. The Secretary of State for Wales, the Director General of Water Services and the National Rivers Authority (NRA) are the principal regulators of the Welsh industry. The Secretary of State and the Minister of Agriculture, Fisheries and Food are responsible for policy relating to land drainage, flood protection, sea defence, and the protection and development of fisheries.

Water resources consist mainly of rainfall stored in upland areas and distributed to the heavily populated valleys and lowland areas. A substantial proportion of the water resources of Wales is used to supply the Midlands and North West of England.

The areas covered by the two water service companies (the principal operating subsidiaries of the water holding companies) which supply Wales are defined by river catchment areas and do not follow the national border with England. Accordingly, Welsh Water (Dwr Cymru Cyfyngedig) includes parts of England on the northern and southern border, while Severn Trent Water, most of whose area is in England, includes the upper Severn Valley in mid-Wales. Besides water supply, these companies are responsible for sewerage and sewage treatment in their areas. Dwr Cymru has a ten-year £1,500 million investment programme, due for completion in the year 2000. It has also spent £25 million in improvements to sewage treatment works.

There are also two supply-only companies—the Wrexham and East Denbighshire, and the Chester—which supply water in parts of north-east Wales. These companies were already in the private sector in 1989.

The report of the Drinking Water Inspectorate in 1991 indicated the high quality of drinking water in Wales. More than 99 per cent of samples taken by the water companies met the requirements of the Water Quality Regulations.

Agriculture, Forestry and Fishing

Agriculture

Agricultural land occupies nearly 1.7 million hectares (4.2 million acres), accounting for about 80 per cent of the area of Wales. It consists mainly of permanent pastures, a significant proportion of which are rough grazings. Because of the relatively poor soil, high rainfall and consequent dependence on livestock rearing, about 80 per cent of the land is designated as 'less favoured areas' by the European Community. The main farming activities within these areas are cattle and sheep rearing, dairying being the most important activity in the better parts of the areas and in the lowlands.

Table 5: Agricultural Production

	1985	1987	1988	1989	1990
Beef ('000 tonnes)	64	72	64	74	72
Sheepmeat ('000 tonnes)	61	67	69	71	71
Pigmeat ('000 tonnes)	17	21	18	18	16
Poultrymeat ('000 tonnes)	56	61	61	60	59
Cereals ('000 tonnes)	311	321	300	315	302
Potatoes ('000 tonnes)	167	155	151	117	132
Oilseed rape ('000 tonnes)	—	33	23	16	23
Milk (million litres)	1,657	1,581	1,535	1,503	1,532
Eggs (millions)	319	315	275	272	286

Source: Welsh Office.

Note: 1990 figures are provisional.

Approximately £170 million, over half of which is funded by the Community, is paid to farmers in Wales as direct support under a range of grants and subsidies. Much of the arable land is used to produce cereals for feeding livestock, but potatoes and other vegetables are important cash crops in many areas, particularly parts of Dyfed.

Output from small farms is more significant than in most of the rest of Britain, but modernisation in agriculture has led to a gradual decrease in the number of small farms and to a reduction in the workforce. In 1991 there were some 3,000 full-time employees, compared with nearly 24,000 in 1961. Some 52,700 people, including farmers, were engaged in agriculture in 1991.

Farmers are encouraged to develop new sources of income as an alternative to surplus production, and through grants, to diversify into tourism and other non-agricultural activities. The Farm Woodland Premium Scheme, introduced in 1992, offers annual payments to farmers who convert land in agricultural use to woodland. The European Community set-aside scheme, introduced in Britain in 1988, provides annual payments to farmers to take their arable land out of agricultural production for five years.

Certain areas of farmland have been designated as Environmentally Sensitive Areas (ESAs). In ESAs, farmers are offered management agreements under which they receive payments (partly reimbursed by the European Community) for following environmentally beneficial farming practices. There are two areas designated as ESAs in Wales: the Cambrian Mountains (Powys and Dyfed) and the Llŷn Peninsula (Gwynedd). Anglesey (Gwynedd) and Radnor (Powys) will be designated as ESAs during 1992–93 and two further areas—Preseli (Dyfed) and the Clwydian Range (Clwyd)—are to be designated in 1993–94.

ADAS Agency, a jointly-run executive agency of the Ministry of Agriculture, Fisheries and Food (MAFF) and the Welsh Office, provides a wide range of consultancy and research services for farmers and growers, ancillary industries and the Government. All services are provided on a fee-paying basis, but through contracts which ADAS has with MAFF and the Welsh Office, growers are able to obtain free initial advice on many aspects. These include conservation of wildlife habitats, rural diversification, animal health and welfare, and measures to protect the environment and to control pollution.

Forestry

About 12 per cent of Wales is covered by woodlands, of which 52 per cent (129,000 hectares—319,000 acres) is administered by the Forest Enterprise.[7] In line with government policy to sell off some of its land to reduce the call on public funds, the Forestry Commission has disposed of some 12,100 hectares (29,800 acres) in Wales since 1981, about 8 per cent of its woodland holdings. Timber production is around 900,000 cubic metres (1.2 million cubic yards) a year.

The Forestry Authority's Woodland Grant Scheme, introduced in June 1991, pays establishment grants to help in the creation of new woodlands and forests, and the regeneration of existing ones. It also pays management grants for silvicultural, environmental and social benefits. As part of the Government's rural initiative for Wales, the Secretary of State launched the

[7]In April 1992 the Forestry Commission was reorganised to make a clear distinction between its two roles. The regulatory and grant-aiding functions as a government department are carried out by the Forestry Authority which also monitors standards for the industry. The Forest Enterprise is responsible for the management of the Commission's forest estate.

Valleys' Forest Initiative which aims to encourage local communities to have a greater involvement in the development of the 35,000 hectares (135 sq miles) of forest in the coalfield valleys of south Wales. Some 1.2 million people live within half an hour's travelling distance of these wooded areas. The Initiative has already resulted in the designation of woodland parks which will increase forest recreation opportunities.

Fishing

Fishing occupies a relatively small place in the economy, with Milford Haven and Holyhead being the largest ports in the Welsh industry. In 1990, 7,000 tonnes of fish, with a value of over £7 million, were landed at Welsh ports. There are 420 commercially active vessels, about 60 per cent of which operate on a part-time basis. Some 370 full-time and 970 part-time fishermen are employed in Wales, with a further 340 onshore workers directly engaged in the industry.

A recent research study estimated the annual value of the Welsh salmon fishery to be in excess of £30 million, making it the most valuable game fishery of the ten regions of the National Rivers Authority.

THE LIBRARY
E R   BURTON COLLEGE
BEVERLEY HU17 8QG
TEL: 0964 550481 Ex: 227

Transport and Communications

Improvements to road and rail links in Wales have played a vital part in the revival of its economy in recent years, and great importance has been attached to ensuring the adequacy of communications between the main centres of population in Wales and the rest of Britain.

Roads

Significant investment has been undertaken through the trunk road programme and expenditure on the roads programme for 1992–93 is £195 million. The completion of the M4 motorway (see map, p. 4 of colour section) will give south Wales much improved access to raw materials and markets in southern England, the Midlands and the North via the national motorway network, assisting the considerable economic recovery of the area. Almost 160 km (100 miles) of continuous motorway and dual carriageway have now been completed between the Severn Bridge and St Clears, Dyfed. A second major motorway crossing of the Severn, costing around £300 million, is under construction, with completion planned for 1996. Under the Severn Bridges Act 1992, the new crossing is being built and will be operated by the private sector (the John Laing/GTM Entrepose consortium). Work on motorway links to the new bridge started in early 1993.

Priority is being given to the improvement of roads which are important for industrial development. For example, the A55 north Wales coast road is being upgraded to dual carriageway standard

Caernarfon Castle. The castles and town walls of King Edward I in Gwynedd were among Britain's first nominations to the World Heritage List. So far 13 sites in Britain have been listed.

The Garden Festival site at Ebbw Vale. The Festival attracted 2 million visitors in 1992.

Two aspects of the development at Cardiff Bay:

The former Penarth Dock, now Penarth Portway Marina.

A former grain warehouse, now refurbished for apartments.

Inward investment has been of particular benefit to Wales. Sony has recently expanded its production facilities at Bridgend.

The British Airways airframe overhaul base under construction at Cardiff-Wales Airport.

Transport

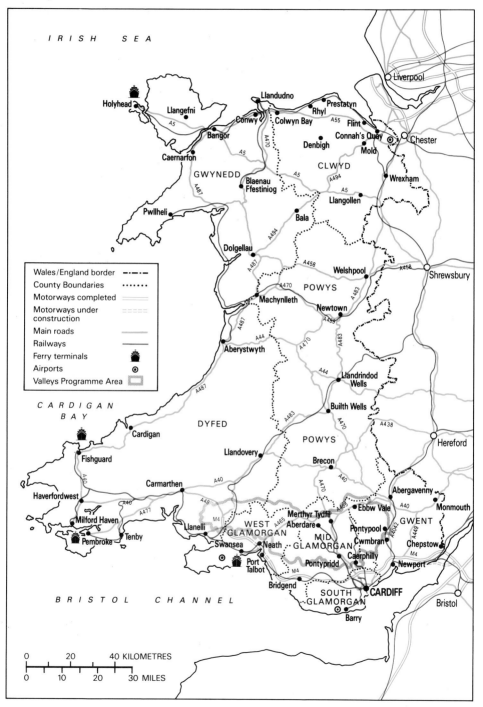

Major Conservation and Recreation Areas

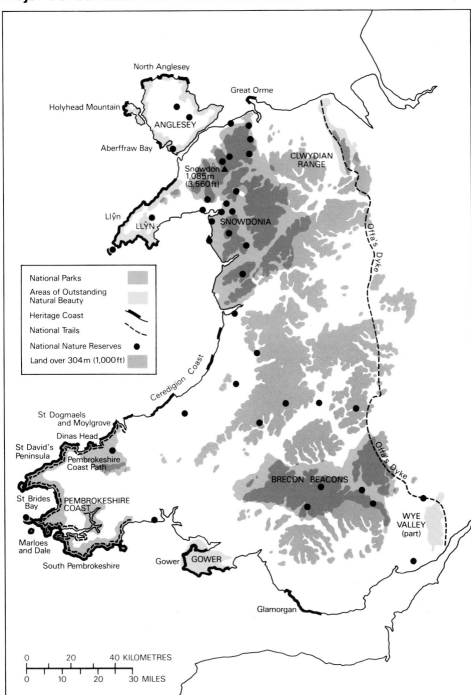

North Anglesey

Great Orme

Holyhead Mountain

ANGLESEY

CLWYDIAN RANGE

Aberffraw Bay

Snowdon ▲ 1,085m (3,560ft)

Llŷn

LLŶN

SNOWDONIA

Offa's Dyke

National Parks

Areas of Outstanding Natural Beauty

Heritage Coast

National Trails

National Nature Reserves ●

Land over 304m (1,000ft)

Ceredigion Coast

St Dogmaels and Moylgrove

Dinas Head

St David's Peninsula

Pembrokeshire Coast Path

Offa's Dyke

St Brides Bay

PEMBROKESHIRE COAST

BRECON BEACONS

WYE VALLEY (part)

Marloes and Dale

South Pembrokeshire

Gower GOWER

Glamorgan

0	20	40 KILOMETRES
0	10	20	30 MILES

Electronics has become increasingly important to the Welsh economy. Here modules are being tested by a company in north Wales which designs systems and makes electronic equipment for business education and training.

The Water Balance Railway at the Centre for Alternative Technology, near Machynlleth.

The new Royal International Pavilion at Llangollen, opened in 1992, is the site for the annual International Music Eisteddfod, which attracts artists from all over the world.

A Plaid Cymru candidate canvassing at the April 1992 General Election. The party now has four MPs, having gained a seat at the election.

Ysbyty George Thomas, a new 100-bed hospital in the Rhondda. It also has a 30-place day centre for the elderly.

In 1992 Colin Jackson achieved considerable success in the 110 metres hurdles, setting a new European record and later winning the event in the World Cup in Havana.

between Bangor and Chester, at a cost of £550 million. Some 57 of the 60 miles are now complete. This includes the construction under the Conwy estuary of the first immersed tube road tunnel to be built in Britain. A tunnel was chosen in preference to a bridge in order to preserve the environment of Conwy Castle and estuary. The tunnel, which is some 1.1 km (0.7 miles) long, was opened in October 1991.

Improvements to the A470 and A483 north–south routes have been carried out, and more are planned. In the south Wales valleys, for example, travelling time from Cardiff to Merthyr Tydfil by car has been cut considerably.

There are about 600 operators of bus services in Wales. Following deregulation of local bus services in 1986, there has been an increase in the number of buses (to around 5,100) and in vehicle mileage operated, with more smaller vehicles operating at greater frequencies.

Rail

InterCity 125 services, operated by British Rail using high speed trains, run on the route linking London, Bristol and south Wales, and also on the cross-country route from south Wales to Birmingham, Sheffield, Leeds and Newcastle upon Tyne. The InterCity service operates through south Wales as far as Fishguard and from London to Holyhead in the north (in both cases linking with ferry services to the Irish Republic). Cross-country express services also run from Cardiff to Birmingham, Liverpool, Manchester, Portsmouth, Shrewsbury and Chester, and other main line services link south, mid and north Wales. Improved rail services are helping to stimulate the economy in the south Wales valleys. Four rail lines have been reopened: the most recent, from

Bridgend to Maesteg, reopened in September 1992. The £4-million programme is funded with support from local authorities and the European Regional Development Fund.

There are a small number of privately run rail lines in Wales. On most of these, steam trains operate, primarily for tourists and railway enthusiasts; they include the Ffestiniog Railway and the Talyllyn Railway. The Vale of Rheidol Railway, which operates on narrow-gauge track between Aberystwyth and Devil's Bridge, was sold by British Rail in 1989 to the Brecon Mountain Railway Company Ltd.

Ports

Traffic through ports in Wales was estimated at 56.4 million tonnes in 1990. Milford Haven, with a deep natural harbour that can take tankers of up to 275,000 deadweight tonnes, is one of Britain's major oil ports and was the fifth largest port in Britain in terms of total tonnage in 1991, when it handled 35.7 million tonnes. Most of the other major ports in south Wales, including Swansea, Port Talbot, Newport, Cardiff and Barry, are run by the privatised company Associated British Ports. Originally they were engaged in coal export, but most now handle a wide range of cargo. Port Talbot handles raw materials (iron ore and coal) destined for the steelworks at Port Talbot and Llanwern, and regularly handles bulk carriers of over 100,000 deadweight tonnes.

Airports

The main civil airport is the Cardiff (Wales) Airport at Rhoose. A number of new air routes to destinations in the rest of Europe have recently been established. The number of terminal passengers in

1991 totalled 513,000, of whom 457,000 were on international services (mainly charter) and 56,000 on domestic services. Traffic has been increasing substantially during 1992–93.

Environment

As in the rest of Britain, there is a comprehensive system of land-use planning and development control in Wales,[8] and there are laws dealing specifically with environmental health, the control of pollution, and the conservation of the natural and built environments. Most development requires planning permission, and applications are dealt with locally in the light of development plans; these set out strategies for each area on such matters as housing, transport, industry and open land. The interests of conservation and those of development and the local economy are balanced carefully when such plans are drawn up.

Programmes of reclamation of land and restoration of buildings in areas left scarred by former industrial development are beginning to transform the environment in, for example, the valleys of south Wales. Developments in urban areas on the coast, such as Swansea and Cardiff, are being planned to take advantage of their natural surroundings, providing new opportunities for leisure as well as economic expansion. Pollution from industrial processes has been considerably reduced in recent years.

The Government's plans for the environment were set out in the 1990 White Paper *This Common Inheritance*. Two annual reports on progress in implementing the plans have been published, the most recent being in October 1992.[9] A separate chapter outlines progress in Wales. Action has been taken in a wide range of

[8]For further information see *Planning* (Aspects of Britain series).
[9]*This Common Inheritance: The Second Year Report*. Cm 2068. HMSO, 1992, £21. ISBN 0 10 120682 8.

areas, including transport, agriculture, the countryside, the urban environment, heritage, energy, and education.

Government priorities for the environment in Wales are:

—to protect and enhance the special landscape and built heritage;

—to enhance controls over pollution and litter;

—to improve further the urban environment by measures including land reclamation and housing improvements; and

—to promote energy efficiency and greater awareness of environmental issues.

Conservation and Environmental Protection

Wales is a country rich in natural beauty, with extensive areas of picturesque hill, lake and mountain country, a fine coastline and many historic towns and villages. The countryside supports a variety of plant and wildlife, which is protected in a number of ways.

Arrangements for protecting the natural environment and encouraging open-air recreation in Wales were altered in April 1991. A new body, the Countryside Council for Wales (CCW), was established to take over the roles in Wales of the former Nature Conservancy Council and the Countryside Commission. It maintains and manages 49 National Nature Reserves in Wales, sites of national importance for study and research into nature conservation, covering some 12,800 hectares (31,600 acres). A Marine Nature Reserve was designated at Skomer, off the coast of Dyfed, in 1990, and consultation is in progress on creating a second reserve in the Menai Strait. Some 841 Sites of Special Scientific Interest (SSSIs) have been listed for their flora, fauna, geological or physiographical features.

Many species are protected under the Wildlife and Countryside Act 1981. Rare species in Wales include the red kite, a bird of prey. The 1992 breeding season was the most successful this century for the red kite in Wales; 79 pairs bred, raising 93 young birds.

The CCW has powers to designate National Parks and Areas of Outstanding Natural Beauty, subject to confirmation by the Secretary of State for Wales; to define heritage coasts in conjunction with local authorities; and to make proposals for the creation of national trails (long-distance footpaths and bridleways).

There are three National Parks (Snowdonia, Brecon Beacons and Pembrokeshire Coast); five Areas of Outstanding Natural Beauty (Gower in West Glamorgan, Llŷn and Anglesey in Gwynedd, the Wye Valley in Gwent and the Clwydian Range in Clwyd); and two national trails (the Pembrokeshire Coast Path and Offa's Dyke Path), as well as 31 country parks and large stretches of heritage coast (see map in colour section). Experimental schemes are under way in National Parks to encourage the maintenance of traditional farming practices, an important aspect of the conservation of the landscape.

Certain areas of farmland have been designated by the Government as Environmentally Sensitive Areas. In these areas farmers are offered financial incentives to maintain the broad pattern of land use (see p. 41). Grants are also available to farmers in all areas to plant new woodlands (see p. 42), and for conservation, anti-pollution and energy-saving devices—for example, for hedges, stone walls, shelter belts, repairs to traditional buildings, and the treatment and disposal of farm wastes.

The Built Environment

Wales has a wide-ranging legacy of ancient monuments and historic buildings. There are, for example, the remains of Roman silver mines in the north and very early ironworks in the south. Small rustic buildings such as those at the Welsh Folk Museum in St Fagans, Cardiff, contrast with the great castles and houses, for example, Caerphilly Castle and Tredegar House, Newport, in south Wales.

A number of statutory, commercial and voluntary bodies work to ensure that the best use is made of the valuable resource that historic buildings and sites of archaeological interest represent. Within the Welsh Office, Cadw: Welsh Historic Monuments, which became an executive agency in 1991, advises the Secretary of State for Wales on matters affecting the built heritage.

Cadw manages 127 historic properties on behalf of the Secretary of State, ranging from ironworks and prehistoric burial chambers to the castles and town walls of King Edward I in Gwynedd (for example, Caernarfon, Harlech, Conwy and Beaumaris). The latter were among Britain's first successful nominations to the World Heritage List, which was established under the World Heritage Convention to identify and recognise those parts of the world heritage of outstanding universal value.

In 1991–92 £1.9 million was spent on the maintenance of Cadw's properties, which were visited in the same year by some 1.4 million people, and accrued income of some £2.4 million. Projects to promote public awareness of these sites include a membership scheme, 'Heritage in Wales', which provides access to all of them.

Another important function of Cadw is the identification and listing of buildings of special historic or architectural interest in order to guide planners, developers and conservation bodies in their work. Some 14,000 historic buildings have already been identified in the Principality. Grants may be made to owners of historic buildings or ancient monuments who need to carry out repairs to ensure their conservation.

As well as restoring historic buildings for commercial purposes—for example, for use as country house hotels—the commercial sector has contributed to the conservation of Wales' built heritage by funding archaeological works and by taking the architecture of the past into account in development proposals. The voluntary sector plays a major role, with many towns in Wales having active civic societies which work to ensure that their local environment is enhanced and the local heritage appreciated (see also below). There are eight National Trust houses open to the public in Wales.

There are also 2,600 scheduled ancient monuments in Wales. Cadw is responsible for exercising the Secretary of State's statutory role in the protection of these sites, and provides advice to owners on their care and preservation.

Voluntary Organisations

There are many voluntary organisations active in the conservation of the natural and built environments in Wales, some of which are large and operate throughout Britain, such as the National Trust and the Royal Society for the Protection of Birds, and others which are local to Wales. Many receive grants from the Government under 'Environment Wales'. The purpose of this initiative is to promote the role of voluntary organisations in conserving and enhancing the environment by providing financial support and encouraging partnerships. The scheme is administered on behalf of the Welsh Office by the Prince of Wales' Committee.

The Association of Trusts for Nature Conservation in Wales, which has seven trusts with more than 9,000 members, helps to protect wildlife by establishing nature reserves and educating people on conservation and environmental issues. The Campaign for the Protection of Rural Wales organises action to protect and improve the rural scenery and amenities of the countryside, towns and villages. The British Trust for Conservation Volunteers has 30 groups in Wales and organises working holidays for volunteers seeking practical experience of conservation work, including tree planting, dry-stone walling and woodland management.

Pollution

Her Majesty's Inspectorate of Pollution (HMIP) has statutory responsibility for the control of pollution in England and Wales, and was formed in 1987 from separate inspectorates, in accordance with the Government's policy of treating the environment as an integrated whole. The Government intends to merge HMIP with the NRA to form a single Environment Agency, and is consulting about how best to do this. A separate Agency is being considered for Wales.

The Environmental Protection Act 1990 introduced a new system of integrated pollution control. This is a single regulatory regime for the most harmful discharges, whether to air, water or land. It is administered in Wales by HMIP. The Act also provides, among other things, for stricter controls over waste disposal and new measures to deal with litter.

Much of Wales is drained by short, steep rivers which are of good quality and have a high amenity value. Many Welsh rivers are also used to provide abstractions for drinking water. Some 94 per cent of the 4,800 km (3,000 miles) of classified rivers and canals in the area of the NRA Welsh Region was classified as of good or fair quality in the 1990 River Quality Survey in England and Wales.

A significant improvement has already been achieved in the quality of Welsh bathing waters; in 1992, 76 per cent met the mandatory coliform bacteria standards of the European Community Bathing Water Directive, compared with 57 per cent in 1987. The NRA Welsh Region is also undertaking studies, with support from the Department of the Environment and the Welsh Office, into the effects of afforestation on river quality, and the consequential impact on fisheries.

Social Developments

Improvements are in hand to tackle the problems of urban areas which have been affected by industrial decline. A number of significant changes are occurring in the housing market. Public provision is made in Wales, as in the rest of Britain, for education at all levels and for a wide range of health and personal social services and social security benefits.

Urban Regeneration

A number of measures have been introduced to assist the regeneration of urban areas which have become derelict as a result of industrial changes. Grants are available to local authorities under the Urban Programme to encourage individual enterprise, help local companies, and improve sites and buildings. Spending on the Urban Programme in Wales is expected to be some £31 million in 1992–93. The 1992–93 programme is targeting the most deprived areas as well as benefiting pockets of deprivation in otherwise prosperous areas.

In 1986 the Welsh Development Agency set up a unit to research, identify and promote opportunities for urban regeneration in Wales. It has established eight priority areas for appropriate action, which can include planning and design, the provision of grants for town improvements, and investment in property development. Projects range from shopping centres and street improvements to landscaping and tourism developments, with the emphasis on establishing effective partnerships between public and private interests. By the end of 1991 the unit had helped to bring a commitment of £93 million of public and private investment to urban regeneration in Wales.

Programme for the Valleys
The south Wales valleys are one of the main areas in Wales to have suffered hardship from the decline of the traditional industries. The Programme for the Valleys, launched in 1988, is the most extensive programme of economic and urban regeneration undertaken in Wales, and covers an area of some 2,200 sq km (860 sq miles) in the south Wales valleys (see map in colour section). It involves increased levels of factory building, land clearance and Urban Programme support, as well as action to stimulate private enterprise; improve health care and educational services; support private housing improvements; and strengthen tourism, the arts and voluntary organisations.

The measures include:

—expansion of the WDA's factory building and urban regeneration programmes, with around 46,000 sq m (500,000 sq ft) of factory space started in 1991–92;

—increased expenditure on the clearance of derelict land, involving the clearance of around 800 hectares (2,000 acres) since 1988, with the aim of virtually eliminating dereliction from the Valleys by the year 2000;

—encouragement for private sector development on derelict and run-down sites by the provision of £21.8 million of Urban Development Grant and Urban Investment Grant from 1988–93;

—higher levels of Urban Programme expenditure, £19.4 million in 1992–93, for projects in the Valleys;

—encouragement for the tourism industry with investment in the Garden Festival of Wales at Ebbw Vale, 1992 (see p. 33);

—some £2.5 million provided for five Valleys communities to participate in Community Revival Strategies, intended to overcome economic, social or environmental deprivation;

—improved facilities for music and the arts;

—investment in housing which led to over 7,000 homes being repaired in the three years to March 1991, with a further 2,850 to be renovated by 1993; and

—over 50 health projects which have been funded or had funding approved to a total of over £25 million.

Cardiff Bay

The Cardiff Bay Development Corporation was set up in 1987 to bring forward redevelopment in an area of south Cardiff, once its commercial centre. By the end of March 1991 the Corporation had received £92 million in government grant. Government support for the Corporation in 1992–93 is £35.1 million. The Corporation's regeneration strategy includes proposals for the construction of a barrage across Cardiff harbour mouth, which would create a large freshwater lake and 12 km (7 miles) of waterside frontage. It is expected that over 23,000 new jobs will be created, 4,400 new homes provided and that over £1,000 million of private investment will be attracted. Road links to the area will also be improved.

The Government is promoting the Cardiff Bay Barrage Bill to achieve these objectives. It is accompanied by a comprehensive environmental statement.

Housing

There is a continuing programme of housing improvement in Wales, which has a higher proportion of old dwellings than any other part of Britain, with almost two-fifths of the dwelling stock having been constructed before 1919, compared with just over a quarter in Great Britain as a whole. Between 1980 and 1990, more than £619 million was spent on grants to enable householders in Wales to repair and improve their homes. The Welsh House Condition Survey of 1988 showed that the state of repair of the housing stock was generally much better than in 1981; the level of unfit dwellings, for example, fell from 8.8 per cent to 7.2 per cent in 1988 and the proportion of dwellings lacking amenities almost halved during this period from 8.1 per cent to 4.2 per cent in 1988.

There is a higher level of owner-occupation in Wales (some 72 per cent at the end of 1991) than in most other parts of Britain (the general average is 68 per cent). Many tenants of public sector housing have taken advantage of the opportunity under the Housing Act 1980 to buy their house or flat at a discount, depending on length of occupation. By March 1992 some 84,650 public sector homes had been sold. In 1991 over 10,300 new dwellings were built in Wales, bringing the number of dwellings to 1.18 million. The private sector accounted for 72 per cent of completions in 1991.

Reform of the rented housing sector was introduced with the Housing Act 1988, which deregulates new lettings in the private rented sector, restructures housing association finance, and offers public sector tenants the opportunity to change their landlord. Under this Act a new housing agency, Housing for Wales (Tai Cymru), was established, to fund and oversee the activities of the housing association movement in Wales, taking over the functions previously carried out by the Housing Corporation based in London.

The housing association movement in Wales has grown to about 100 associations, managing some 24,000 dwellings, and the

Government expects it to be the major provider of social rented housing for the future. While the Government is allocating £123 million in funding for Housing for Wales in 1992–93, the number of new homes provided will also be increased by the use of private finance to help fund housing association schemes. Their target has been increased to 3,500 new homes in 1992–93. Housing associations are being particularly encouraged to provide low-cost housing in rural areas; where there is a need for this, sites for which planning permission would not normally be granted for general housing development may be released by the planning authorities.

A Charter for Council Tenants in Wales was published in September 1992. It explains tenants' legal rights, how they can be exercised, where to get more information, and what to do if things go wrong. Approval was also given in 1992 for the issue by Housing for Wales of a new Tenants' Guarantee for housing association tenants.

Education

The Welsh Office is responsible for non-university education. Schools and further education colleges are administered by eight local government education authorities which are funded by central and local tax revenue. The Welsh Office funds the non-university institutions of higher education and is consulted about university education. From 1 April 1993 responsibility for funding the whole of the higher education sector in Wales will rest with the Higher Education Funding Council for Wales.

Schools

In 1991 there were 270,000 pupils in Welsh primary schools and 185,000 in secondary schools. The average numbers of pupils per teacher were 22.3 and 15.4 respectively.

Welsh and English are both used as media of instruction in a number of schools. Most Welsh-medium schools are situated in the traditionally Welsh-speaking, largely rural areas. There are also designated bilingual schools in the anglicised, mainly industrial areas to cater for children whose parents wish them to be educated through the medium of both languages. Welsh is a core subject in Welsh-speaking schools and a foundation subject elsewhere under the National Curriculum. The National Curriculum requirements for Welsh were introduced in 1990.

The other core subjects are English, mathematics and science; foundation subjects include history, geography, technology, music, art, physical education and—for secondary school pupils—a modern foreign language. Statutory assessments are made of pupils' progress at ages 7, 11, 14 and 16 in order to measure achievement against national standards. Parents of pupils receive a yearly progress report on their child's National Curriculum achievements and results in public examinations. The National Record of Achievement, launched in 1991, is a record of achievement in education and training designed for use throughout working life.

Religious education is required for all pupils as part of the basic curriculum. Parents have a right to withdraw their children from religious education classes.

The Curriculum Council for Wales advises the Secretary of State on the curriculum and provides advice and guidance to teachers. The National Curriculum places a strong emphasis on information technology, and the cross-curricular use of educational technology is being encouraged so that pupils become familiar with the new technologies and use them to enhance learning. The average number of pupils per microcomputer fell between 1988 and 1991 from 68 to 34 in primary schools and from 30 to 14 in secondary schools. The Welsh Office has funded the provision of satellite broadcast receiving equipment, now installed in nearly all secondary schools.

Secondary, as well as larger primary, schools are responsible for managing most of their budgets, including staffing costs. All schools will have these delegated powers by April 1995. Following a ballot of parents giving consent, schools can also apply to become grant-maintained and withdraw from control by the local education authority; they would then be funded directly from the Welsh Office.

In September 1991 the Government published *Education: A Charter for Parents in Wales* as part of the Citizen's Charter initiative. It sets out the rights of parents with respect to the education of their children: the choices they can exercise; the information they can obtain about schools' performance; and the influence they can have on the way schools are run.

The Government encourages more schools to offer vocational qualifications which it regards as an equally valid route to further and higher education and training. It considers that co-operation between the education system and business is essential. As a result of the Government's Technical and Vocational Education Initiative and other measures, industrial and commercial matters are being given greater attention in school, college and university curricula and examinations. The aim is to make the curriculum more practical by developing business skills and the use of information technology. Businessmen and women are involved in curriculum development and enterprise activities for schoolchildren. They are also represented in greater numbers on school and college governing bodies.

All school-leavers aged 16 or 17 not wishing to go on to further and higher education or directly into employment are offered one-year or two-year training placements in industry.

Post-school Education

About 47 per cent of young people receive some form of post-school education; 14 per cent of 18-year-olds are in higher education. There has been an increase in the numbers of those enrolling for both higher and further education. Enrolments for non-university higher education rose by 17 per cent in 1991–92 to 28,000 and for further education by 2 per cent to 85,800. In 1991–92 there were 29,500 students at the six constituent colleges of the University of Wales—University College, Aberystwyth; University College of North Wales, Bangor; University of Wales College of Cardiff; University College of Swansea; University of Wales College of Medicine, Cardiff; and St David's University College, Lampeter. In September 1992 the Polytechnic of Wales, at Treforest, became the University of Glamorgan.[10]

The Universities Funding Council allocates funds to the university colleges. Its Welsh Committee ensures that Welsh issues are taken into account. The Government has established a new Higher Education Funding Council for Wales which will assume responsibility for allocating public funds to the university colleges and the other Welsh higher education institutions.

Local education authorities are responsible for funding their further education colleges. Further education and sixth-form colleges will become autonomous institutions free from local authority control from April 1993 when they will be funded by the Further Education Council for Wales. The Council will distribute funds provided by the Government with an additional element related to student numbers. Colleges will be free to employ their own staff and manage their own resources.

[10]Legislation passed in 1992 has been designed to transform post-compulsory education and training. The reforms have ended the distinction between universities, polytechnics and other higher education establishments. For further information see *Education* (Aspects of Britain series).

The Government's LINK programme is encouraging industry to undertake joint research with higher education institutions. There are science parks at Aberystwyth, Bangor, Swansea and the North East Wales Institute of Higher Education. Set up by these institutions together with industrial scientists, their purpose is to promote the development and commercial application of advanced technology and academic research. A new science park, Imperial Park, is being constructed in Newport as a joint venture between the Welsh Development Agency, Newport Borough Council, and Imperial College, London. It will provide space for high-technology companies based around a technological research centre, with voice, data and video links to Imperial College.

Health

The National Health Service (NHS) in Wales is provided through the Welsh Office, which has a general strategic planning responsibility, and by nine district health authorities. The services are designed to promote improvement in people's health through the prevention, diagnosis and treatment of illness. Provision is being made to meet the increasing requirement for health care of the growing number of elderly people, to introduce new treatments, and to provide community care for those not needing continuing hospital care. Increasing emphasis is being given to the promotion of good health and the extension of preventive measures—for example, to combat problems such as coronary heart disease, cancer, AIDS and the misuse of drugs and alcohol. A special health authority has been established to develop this work.

Spending on the NHS in Wales has risen by almost 49 per cent in real terms over the last decade. This has been complemented by improved efficiency and management: in the period 1985–86 to 1990–91 cumulative efficiency savings by the district health authorities amounted to £55.1 million. In 1990–91 £1,501 million was spent on health services, of which over £1,077 million was on hospital and community health services. Over 50 development schemes worth some £380 million are at various stages of planning and construction.

Some 3,100 staff are contracted to work for the family health services authorities, of whom about 1,800 are general practitioners (GPs). The average number of patients on each doctor's list is around 1,800 (the average for Britain is about 1,910). An increasing proportion of family doctors work in modern, well-equipped health centres, where they form part of a medical and nursing team; dental, social work and other services may also be provided in the centres. By April 1992 over 150 GPs had become fundholders (with responsibility for their own budgets), covering nearly 300,000 patients. A further 230 GPs in some 50 practices are preparing to join the scheme in April 1993.

There have been substantial increases in the number of primary health-care staff in recent years. For example, the number of dentists rose by 36 per cent between 1979 and 1991, family doctors by 24 per cent and opticians by 39 per cent. A nationwide breast cancer screening service is being introduced for all women aged between 50 and 65. In Wales all eligible women should have their mammography screening invitations by 1993. All Welsh district health authorities are now running a computerised call and recall service for cervical screening, which enables all women aged between 20 and 64 to be invited regularly for screening.

In Wales in 1990–91, NHS hospitals provided some 19,400 beds and the NHS had some 30,800 directly employed medical, dental, nursing and midwifery staff. The hospital service is now treating more patients than ever before. During 1991–92 district health authorities treated a record 630,000 in-patient and day cases,

9 per cent more than in 1990–91. Length of stay for in-patients has declined, while advances in medical technology and practice have resulted in a large increase in the number of people being treated as day cases; in 1991–92 some 129,000 day cases were treated. In 1992–93 £1 million is being allocated to support action to reduce waiting times for treatment.

The health of the population in Wales is continuing to improve. Perinatal mortality fell from 14.1 per 1,000 births in 1981 to 7.9 per 1,000 in 1991, and infant mortality fell from 12.6 per 1,000 live births in 1981 to 6.6 per 1,000 in 1991. By 1989 life expectancy for both men and women had increased by three years compared with 1979 (to 72 and 78 years respectively). The prevalence of cigarette smoking has fallen, as elsewhere in Great Britain, with a reduction in Wales from 46 per cent of people aged 16 or over in 1974 to 31 per cent in 1990.

As part of the Programme for the Valleys (see p. 56), further government investment has been made in hospitals, health centres and in schemes to assist elderly people, and to improve primary health care, ante-natal care, and the treatment of patients with heart problems in the south Wales valleys. Nearly £26 million has been invested in health care, and 53 schemes have benefited.

The National Health Service and Community Care Act 1990 has introduced wide-ranging reform in management and patient care in the health and social care services. The NHS reforms, which came into effect in 1991, aim to give patients, wherever they live in Britain, better health care and greater choice of service. While the NHS continues to be open to all regardless of income, there has been greater delegation of decision-making and financial responsibility to hospitals and general practices at local level.

Personal Social Services

The personal social services are administered and funded mainly by local authorities, and provide advice, care and support for the most vulnerable members of the community. The demand for personal social services is expected to rise over the next few years, owing to the increasing number of elderly people and the changing pattern of care for people with a mental handicap, those with a mental illness, and those who are chronically sick.

The Government's policy, under its general programme 'Care in the Community', is that care for vulnerable groups should be provided as far as possible in the community rather than in large institutions. The recent reforms in community care provision, which take effect between April 1991 and April 1993, establish a new financial and managerial framework, and are intended to enable vulnerable groups in the community to live as normal a life as possible in their own homes and to give them a greater say in how they live and how the services they need should be provided. Some £36 million will be available in 1993–94 for local authorities to meet the cost of their new community care responsibilities.

The Welsh Office's 10-year mental health strategy, which began in 1983, aims to develop a comprehensive range of services for people with a mental handicap, to enable them to lead independent lives, in normal surroundings, in their own communities. In order to help develop these facilities, the Welsh Office is providing direct financial support in response to joint plans produced by health and social services authorities (in addition to their own resources) and to voluntary organisations. Provision for direct support in 1992–93 is £41.5 million. The Secretary of State has decided to relaunch the strategy from April 1993 following the end of the first 10-year phase. Similarly, the mental illness strategy is promoting new patterns of locally based care to meet comprehensively the needs of people with a mental illness in a way that ends reliance on traditional mental hospitals. Levels of Welsh Office funding (£6 million in 1992–93) will be decided in the light of plans being jointly developed by local health, social service and voluntary agencies in consultation with those using the services. A key feature of the new services is the central role of community mental health teams.

The Welsh Office's 'Care of the Elderly Initiative' has helped to fund nearly 60 demonstration projects aimed at stimulating developments in the provision of care for elderly people. This was superseded by the new Flexible Community Care Grant Scheme introduced in 1991–92 to promote more flexible forms of community care for the elderly and for disabled people—including carers—through, and in funding partnership with, local authorities and voluntary bodies.

Local authorities also make provision for services for children and young people, people with physical disabilities, for those suffering from mental illness, and for people with a learning disability. The voluntary sector makes an important contribution in, for example, the day care of pre-school children, and the private sector is providing a growing number of places in residential care homes, mainly for the elderly.

Local authorities also have important responsibilities for the care and protection of children and young people. With the benefit of direct government grant, local authorities are increasing programmes of training for social workers and others caring for children at risk. Generally local authorities' child care policies give priority to maintaining children within their own families or, where necessary, providing family care within the community. Some children are cared for in residential homes, but these numbers are decreasing.

THE LIBRARY
BISHOP BURTON COLLEGE
BEVERLEY HU17 8QG
TEL: 0964 550481 Fx· 227

Language and Culture

Language

Welsh is a language belonging to the Celtic family, its nearest
cousins being Cornish (now extinct) and Breton. The language as
spoken today is descended directly from Early Welsh, which
emerged as a distinct tongue as early as the sixth century. It is thus
the oldest living language of Britain and among the oldest in
Europe. It has a rich and varied literature, stretching from medieval
times to the present day, particularly distinguished by the poetic
tradition.

At the start of the twentieth century 50 per cent of the population of Wales were able to speak Welsh, according to the 1901
census. The numbers speaking Welsh, however, have continued to
decline sharply since then. At the time of the 1991 census Welsh
speakers made up 19 per cent of the population. The distribution of
the language is uneven, however, and in much of rural north and
west Wales Welsh remains the first language of most of the population (between 58 per cent and 75 per cent). By contrast, only 6.5 per
cent of the population of South Glamorgan spoke Welsh in 1991,
and 2.4 per cent in Gwent.

Since the 1960s, however, both the Government and voluntary groups have taken steps to revive the use of Welsh. The Welsh
Language Act 1967 guaranteed the right to use Welsh in court, and
provided for its use in public administration. There are now many
more bilingual publications and official forms than previously, and
most road signs are bilingual. There is some evidence that the

decline in the number of Welsh speakers is now being halted, with increasing numbers of children and young people able to speak Welsh.

The Welsh Language Board
In 1988 the Government announced the establishment of a Welsh Language Board to advise the Secretary of State on matters relating to the Welsh language. Its tasks have included:

—developing voluntary codes of practice on the use of Welsh in the public and private sectors;

—advising on the use of Welsh in public administration;

—investigating complaints;

—reviewing and reporting on grant-supported activity; and

—liaising with statutory and non-statutory bodies on language issues.

The Board works through specialist sub-committees which have concentrated on the promotion of the Welsh language, the use of the Welsh language by local authorities and public bodies, its use in the private sector, and proposals for legislation. Its projects include the Iaith Gwaith (Working Welsh) scheme, which some 600 workplaces have adopted, and the commissioning of University College, Bangor, to develop CYSILL, a Welsh-language spell-check software package.

The Government has announced higher grants, amounting to £7.6 million, in support of the Welsh language in 1992–93.

Welsh Language Bill
The Government has put forward proposals for a Welsh Language Bill, based on recommendations made by the Board. The Bill is

designed to ensure that Welsh speakers are able to use Welsh when dealing with public authorities. It would place a duty on councils and public agencies in Wales to draw up schemes defining the services they provide for Welsh speakers. These schemes would be agreed by the Board, and would be placed on a statutory footing. It would also amend legislation which has been seen as granting a lesser status to Welsh than to English in Wales.

Welsh Language Education
Support for bilingual education has been reflected in the numbers of pupils learning Welsh at primary and secondary school level. Welsh constitutes a core subject in Welsh-speaking schools and a foundation subject elsewhere under the National Curriculum (see p. 60). About a third of schools teach some or all subjects through the medium of Welsh.

Since 1980, the Government has been providing grants for projects which extend or improve the quality of education in the Welsh language. About £4.6 million is available to support developments in Welsh language education in 1992–93. Priority in the allocation of this funding is given to projects which support the introduction of Welsh under the National Curriculum. One of the principal activities supported is the work of the teams of Athrawon Bro (area teachers), mobile forces of experienced Welsh language teachers in each local education authority, who assist schools and teachers with teaching Welsh. Other projects include centres which provide intensive language coaching for children moving to Welsh speaking areas, residential courses for children, and support for schemes aimed at teaching Welsh to adults.

There are opportunities for studying the Welsh language and for studying through the medium of Welsh in the institutions of further and higher education, including the University of Wales. In many further education colleges A-level courses in Welsh and an increasing range of bilingual courses in vocational subjects are offered, while at some of the colleges of higher education all or part of some degree and higher national diploma courses, mainly with a vocational emphasis, may be taken through the medium of Welsh. Postgraduate and undergraduate courses training both primary and secondary teachers are provided through the medium of Welsh in the university colleges and colleges of higher education in the Welsh-speaking areas (Aberystwyth, Bangor and Carmarthen).

Other Welsh Language Initiatives

Radio and television programmes in Welsh are broadcast regularly; on the fourth television channel, Sianel Pedwar Cymru (S4C), established in 1982, a substantial proportion of the programmes are in Welsh (see p. 73). Some local newspapers and other publications are printed wholly or partly in Welsh.

Official grants have been made to the Welsh-language play-group movement (catering for 'pre-school' children under five), to the Royal National Eisteddfod of Wales (see p. 72), to Urdd Gobaith Cymru (the Welsh League of Youth), and to the Welsh Books Council, which administers grants to Welsh language publishers and runs promotion projects such as a children's book club.

Culture

There is much cultural activity in Wales, especially in literature, drama and music. Two of the major annual professional arts festivals are held at Swansea and St David's Hall (Cardiff), and numerous amateur festivals, known as eisteddfodau, are held regularly. As an institution the Eisteddfod can be traced back for centuries, but in its modern form it dates back to the late nineteenth century when a conscious effort to revive it was made. The largest of these festivals is the Royal National Eisteddfod of Wales, which was instituted in 1880 as part of a systematic attempt to preserve Welsh traditional culture. Competitions in music, singing, prose and poetry take place, and proceedings are conducted entirely in Welsh. The town of Llangollen (Clwyd) has extended its Eisteddfod to include artists from all over the world in an annual international folk festival. The Urdd Gobaith Cymru (Welsh League of Youth) Eisteddfod is the largest youth festival in Europe.

The founding of the National Library of Wales and the National Museum of Wales at the beginning of the present century was closely connected with the revival of the National Eisteddfod. More recently the promotion of cultural activities has become the responsibility of the Welsh Arts Council. Wales is famed for its choral singing (especially male-voice choirs), and the Welsh National Opera, formed in 1945 and based in Cardiff, has gained an international reputation.

The literature of Wales ranges from the folk tales of the Mabinogion and legends about King Arthur to the work of modern writers in which traditional influences are often very strong. Noted twentieth-century writers include W.H. Davies, Richard Llewellyn, Dylan Thomas and R.S. Thomas. Leading writers in Welsh include T. Gwyn Jones, Sir Thomas Parry-Williams, Saunders Lewis, Kate Roberts, R. Williams Parry and Sir Thomas Parry.

Prominent painters have included Richard Wilson, Augustus John, Ceri Richards and Kyffin Williams. Numerous famous performers in the fields of theatre, cinema, light entertainment, music and opera have included Richard Burton, Emlyn Williams,

Margaret Price, Sir Geraint Evans, Dame Gwyneth Jones, Sir Harry Secombe and Sir Anthony Hopkins.

Wales is a flourishing centre for crafts, with an increasing number of people taking an interest in the traditional crafts in wool such as spinning, dyeing, knitting and weaving, or in others such as pottery, woodturning, and toymaking. Many small businesses based on crafts with appeal to tourists have become established in rural areas. In 1988 the Government launched the Welsh Craft Initiative, designed to highlight the distinctive identity of Welsh craft products and to co-ordinate their marketing and promotion.

The fourth television channel, Sianel Pedwar Cymru (S4C), broadcasts most of its programmes in Welsh during peak viewing hours and is required to see that a significant amount of programming, in practice 23 hours a week, is in Welsh. The establishment of S4C and the continued encouragement of the Welsh language have done much for the development of the arts in the language, with increased opportunities for writers in Welsh and for Welsh-speaking actors. Cinema-going is popular too; Cardiff is one of the most active film and television production centres in Britain, after London, particularly in the field of animation, where companies like Siriol have a worldwide reputation.

Planned expenditure by the Government on the arts and libraries in Wales is £22.9 million in 1992–93, which includes an allocation of some £14 million to the National Museum of Wales in Cardiff where a major expansion scheme is in progress at the main building in Cathays Park. The scheme, costing £21.2 million, is designed to produce new galleries, improved storage areas and greatly enhanced facilities for visitors. The project is scheduled for completion in 1992–93. The Museum has a number of branches, including the Welsh Folk Museum at St Fagans, near Cardiff; the

Industrial and Maritime Museum in Cardiff's dockland; the Museum of the Woollen Industry at Drefach Felindre (Dyfed); and the Museum of the North at Llanberis (Gwynedd). The National Library of Wales at Aberystwyth contains some 2.5 million printed books and is one of six copyright libraries entitled to claim copies of material printed in Britain. It is also an archive depository holding a major manuscript collection of both official and private records relating to Wales.

Under the Government's Programme for the Valleys (see p. 56), a number of improved centres for the arts are being provided in the south Wales valleys, with the refurbishment of existing buildings such as the Parc and Dare Hall at Treorchy, the Coliseum Theatre, Trecynon and a number of workmen's halls. A large project at Ystradgynlais, to provide the upper Swansea valley and south-west Powys with a suitable venue for the performing arts, has also been approved.

Sport and Recreation

A wide range of sports and recreational activities, both indoor and outdoor, are popular in Wales, although levels of participation are estimated to be below the British average. However, in recent years they have risen, because of more leisure time, increased provision of leisure facilities, and rising living standards. Much of this increased participation has been in individual activities such as jogging, swimming, aerobics and weight training. In 1991–92, 47 per cent of the population of Wales aged 15 and over participated in sport and physical recreation. The most popular sporting activities in Wales include swimming, walking, jogging, cycling, snooker, football and badminton.

Association football is the most widely played team sport. There are three professional clubs playing in the Football League (which covers England and Wales) and nearly 2,000 amateur clubs. Rugby union football has come to be regarded as the Welsh national game. Some of the leading clubs, such as Cardiff, Swansea, Pontypool and Llanelli, are known throughout the rugby-playing world. In 1983 the Welsh Rugby Union completed the modernisation of the National Stadium at Cardiff Arms Park. More than 50 other sports and games are played in Wales, including athletics, gymnastics, hockey and cricket.

In 1987–88 Wales had 26 performers who became British champions; by 1990–91 this figure had risen to 53. In 1991 Ian Woosnam won the United States Masters golf tournament and at the beginning of 1992 he was ranked number one in the world. In the 1988 Olympic Games the Welsh athlete Colin Jackson won a silver medal for Britain in the 110 m hurdles. He subsequently won the gold medal at this event in the 1990 Commonwealth Games and in the 1990 European Championships, and won the event in the 1992 World Cup. Wales competes as a national team in the Commonwealth Games, and in the 1990 Games in Auckland (New Zealand) Welsh competitors won a total of 25 medals: 10 gold, 3 silver and 12 bronze. Sport for disabled people has developed rapidly in recent years and Welsh athletes competed at the Barcelona Paralympics in 1992.

The mountainous area of the Snowdonia National Park in north Wales and other upland areas such as the Brecon Beacons are naturally suited to outdoor activities such as hill-walking, mountaineering and pony-trekking, and the long coastline gives many opportunities for sea-bathing and sailing.

Angling (game, coarse and sea) is the most popular outdoor sporting activity in Wales. Wales has extensive salmon and sea trout fisheries, including some famous salmon rivers such as the Wye, Usk, Teifi, Conwy and Dee, while the rivers Tywi, Dovey, Mawddach, and Dwyfor are equally well known for the abundance and size of their 'sewin' (sea trout). The main centres for fishing for non-migratory trout and other freshwater fish are the lakes and reservoirs.

The Sports Council for Wales

The Sports Council for Wales, a government-financed agency, is responsible for assisting the development of sport in Wales. It aims to increase participation in sport, to encourage high standards of performance, to advise on the planning and provision of facilities, and to disseminate information and advice. It receives a government grant, which amounted to £5.8 million in 1992–93. The Council provides grants to voluntary sports clubs for capital development, training and competition. A new series of local sports development grants was launched in 1990–91.

In 1986 the Council launched a ten-year strategy for sport in Wales, covering the period 1986–96. In June 1991 it published a strategy review, *Changing Times: Changing Needs*, which updated the original strategy. As a priority there are three objectives:

—to increase participation in sport by concentrating on young people;

—to provide more local community sports facilities by adapting existing school facilities in the areas of greatest need; and

—to raise the standard of performances through improved teaching provision and improved effectiveness of sports' governing bodies.

The Sports Council for Wales is also responsible for administering the two national sports centres:

—the Welsh Institute for Sport, which is a mainly indoor centre in Cardiff—it held 193 major events in 25 sports in 1990–91; and

—the Plas Menai National Watersports Centre, near Caernarfon.

A third national centre, the National Centre for Mountain Activities, is operated by the Sports Council[11] at Plas y Brenin in north Wales. In addition, the British Canoe Union, through agreement with Welsh Water, manages Canolfan Tryweryn, a National White Water Canoe Centre at Bala.

Other Organisations

The local authorities are important providers of recreational facilities for public use. They provide parks, playing fields, swimming

[11]This refers to the Sports Council, which has responsibility for general sporting matters affecting Great Britain.

pools, indoor sports halls and tennis courts. Provision of such facilities has been increasing. For example, the number of indoor sports halls in Wales grew from 11 in 1972 to 120 in 1991. Similarly the number of swimming pools rose from 25 to 114 over the same period. While many of these facilities are in urban areas, the Sports Council for Wales has assisted provision in rural areas by encouraging the use of education facilities and upgrading village halls to enable them to be used for sport.

The Welsh Sports Association, which the Sports Council for Wales consults, represents the governing bodies of sport in Wales. The Association works closely with other bodies with responsibility for sport and recreation. The Countryside Council for Wales, in addition to its conservation responsibilities, is concerned with the planning and provision of recreational facilities in the countryside.

Addresses

Welsh Office, Cathays Park, Cardiff CF1 3NQ; and Gwydyr House, Whitehall, London SW1A 2ER.

Ancient Monuments Board for Wales, Brunel House, 2 Fitzalan Road, Cardiff CF2 1UY.

Cadw: Welsh Historic Monuments, Brunel House, 2 Fitzalan Road, Cardiff CF2 1UY.

Cardiff Bay Development Corporation, Baltic House, Mount Stuart Square, Cardiff CF1 6DH.

Countryside Council for Wales, Plas Penrhos, Ffordd Penrhos, Bangor, Gwynedd LL57 2LQ.

The Development Board for Rural Wales, Ladywell House, Newtown, Powys SY16 1JB.

Land Authority for Wales, Custom House, Custom House Street, Cardiff CF1 5AP.

National Library of Wales, Aberystwyth, Dyfed SY23 3BU.

National Museum of Wales, Cathays Park, Cardiff CF1 3NP.

Royal Commission on Ancient and Historical Monuments in Wales, Crown Building, Plas Crug, Aberystwyth, Dyfed SY23 2HP.

Sports Council for Wales, The National Sports Centre for Wales, Sophia Gardens, Cardiff CF1 9SW.

Wales Tourist Board, Brunel House, 2 Fitzalan Road, Cardiff CF2 1UY.

Welsh Arts Council, 9 Museum Place, Cardiff CF1 3NS.

Welsh Development Agency, Pearl House, Greyfriars Road, Cardiff CF1 3XX.

Welsh Water, Cambrian Way, Brecon, Powys LD3 7HP.

Further Reading

£

BALSOM, Denis. *The Wales Yearbook.*
                              Gwasg Gomer

COLE, David. *The New Wales.*
ISBN 0 7083 1087 7.   University of Wales Press   1990   25.00

GEORGE, K.D. and MAINWARING, Lynn.
The Welsh Economy.
ISBN 0 7083 1015 X.   University of Wales Press   1988   35.00

WILLIAMS, Glanmor. *The Welsh and Their*
Religion: Historical Essays.
ISBN 0 7083 1097 4.   University of Wales Press   1991   27.50

Education: A Charter for Parents in
Wales.   Welsh Office   1991   Free

Health: A Charter for Patients in
Wales.   Welsh Office   1991   Free

Housing in Wales: An Agenda for
Action.   Welsh Office   1991   Free

Review of Educational Provision in
Wales 1991–92.   Welsh Office   1992   Free

The Structure of Local Government
in Wales.   Welsh Office   1991   Free

The Valleys: A Programme for
the People. . .   Welsh Office   1988   Free

£

The Valleys: A Partnership for
the People . . .   Welsh Office   1990   Free
The Welsh Language: A Strategy for the
Future.   Welsh Language Board   1989   Free

Select Committee Reports and Government Responses
Affordable Housing. 5th Report of the
Welsh Affairs Committee, Session 1990–91.
Vol. 1. Report. ISBN 0 10 028969 X.   HMSO   1991   8.90

Vol. 2. Minutes of Evidence and Appendices
ISBN 0 10 028999 1.   HMSO   1991   22.00

Affordable Housing. The Government's Response
to the 5th Report of the Welsh Affairs
Committee, Session 1990–91. Cm 1793.
ISBN 0 10 117932 4.   HMSO   1992   2.90

Cardiff–Wales Airport. First Report of the
Welsh Affairs Committee, Session 1990–91.
ISBN 0 10 216691 9.   HMSO   1991   9.60

Community Care: the Elderly. 4th Report
of the Welsh Affairs Committee, Session 1991–92.
Vol. 1. Report. ISBN 0 10 216092 9.   HMSO   1992   12.95

Vol. 2. Minutes of Evidence and Appendices.
ISBN 0 10 291492 3.   HMSO   1992   27.30

Creating and Safeguarding Jobs in
Wales. House of Commons Committee of
Public Accounts Fifth Report,
Session 1992–93. ISBN 0 10 207693 6.   HMSO   1992   13.35

£

Elective Surgery. 6th Report of the Welsh
Affairs Committee, Session 1990–91.
Vol 1. Report. ISBN 0 10 028979 7.   HMSO   1991   7.95

Vol 2. Minutes of Evidence and Appendices.
ISBN 0 10 028989 4.   HMSO   1991   24.80

*The Future of Opencast Coalmining in
Wales.* 2nd Report of the Welsh Affairs
Committee, Session 1990–91.
Vol. 1. Report. ISBN 0 10 284991 9.   HMSO   1991   7.85

Vol. 2. Minutes of Evidence and Appendices.
ISBN 0 10 286091 2.   HMSO   1991   16.10

Rail Services in Wales. 4th Report of the
Welsh Affairs Committee, Session 1990–91.
ISBN 0 10 226291 8.   HMSO   1991   11.85

Rail Services in Wales. The Government
Response to the Welsh Affairs Committee
Report. Cm 1785. ISBN 0 10 157852 2.   HMSO   1991   1.90

Roads in Wales. First Report of the Welsh
Affairs Committee, Session 1991–92.
ISBN 0 10 208992 2.   HMSO   1992   9.75

Roads in Wales. Government Response to the
First Report of the Welsh Affairs Committee,
Session 1991–92. Cm 1851.
ISBN 0 10 118512 X.   HMSO   1992   1.50

Periodical Publications
Annual publication available from the relevant body, except where
stated.

Cardiff Bay Development Corporation.

Countryside Council for Wales.

Development Board for Rural Wales.

Digest of Welsh Statistics.   HMSO

The Government's Expenditure Plans:
A Report by the Welsh Office.   HMSO

Housing for Wales.

The Sports Council for Wales.

Wales Tourist Board.

Welsh Development Agency.

Welsh Economic Trends. Biennial.   Welsh Office

Welsh Social Trends. Biennial.   Welsh Office

Index

Printed in the UK for HMSO.
Dd.0295748, 3/93, C30, 51-2423, 5673.

A MONTHLY UPDATE

ASPECTS OF BRITAIN

Current Affairs
a monthly survey

September 1992 Vol 22 No 9

London Conference on Former Yugoslavia
Outcome of the EC/UN Peace Conference

Balance of Payments 1991
Balance of Payments 'Pink Book'

Iraq
Deployment of Allied Military Aircraft over Southern Iraq

Research and Development
The Government's Annual Review of R & D

Regional Trends
Analysis of Regional Contrasts in Britain

CURRENT AFFAIRS:
A MONTHLY SURVEY

Using the latest authoritative information from official and other sources, *Current Affairs* is an invaluable digest of important developments in all areas of British affairs. Focusing on policy initiatives and other topical issues, its factual approach makes it the ideal companion for *Britain Handbook* and *Aspects of Britain*. Separate sections deal with governmental; international; economic; and social, cultural and environmental affairs. A further section provides details of recent documentary sources for these areas. There is also a twice-yearly index.

Annual subscription including index and postage £35·80 net.
Binder £4·95.

Buyers of Britain 1993: An Official Handbook *qualify for a discount of 25 per cent on a year's subscription to* Current Affairs *(see next page)*.

HMSO Publications Centre
(Mail and telephone orders only)
PO Box 276
LONDON SW8 5DT
Telephone orders: 071 873 9090

THE ANNUAL PICTURE

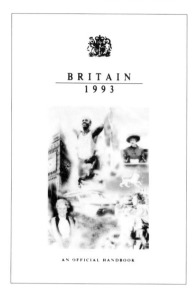

BRITAIN
1993

AN OFFICIAL HANDBOOK

BRITAIN HANDBOOK

The annual picture of Britain is provided by *Britain: An Official Handbook* - the forty-fourth edition will be published early in 1993. It is the unrivalled reference book about Britain, packed with information and statistics on every facet of British life.

With a circulation of over 20,000 worldwide, it is essential for libraries, educational institutions, business organisations and individuals needing easy access to reliable and up-to-date information, and is supported in this role by its sister publication, *Current Affairs: A Monthly Survey*.

Approx. 500 pages; 24 pages of colour illustrations; 16 maps; diagrams and tables throughout the text; and a statistical section. Price £19·50.

Buyers of Britain 1993: An Official Handbook *have the opportunity of a year's subscription to* Current Affairs *at 25 per cent off the published price of £35·80. They will also have the option of renewing their subscription next year at the same discount. Details in each copy of* Handbook, *from HMSO Publications Centre and at HMSO bookshops (see back of title page).*

THE LIBRARY
BISHOP BURTON COLLEGE
BEVERLEY HU17 8QG
TEL: 0964 550481 Ex: 227